The BIG ILLINOIS Activity Book!

BY CAROLE MARSH

This activity book has material which correlates with
the Illinois Learning Standards.

At every opportunity, we have tried to relate information to
the History and Social Science, English, Science, Math, Civics,
Economics, and Computer Technology ILS directives.

For additional information, go to our websites:
www.illinoisexperience.com or **www.gallopade.com**.

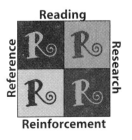

The Big Activity Book Team

Billie Walburn

Michael Marsh

Debra Sims

Michele Yother

Carole Marsh

Bob Longmeyer

William Nesbitt, Jr.

Steven Saint-Laurent

Sue Gentzke

Sherry Moss

Cecil Anderson

Chad Beard

Jennifer McGann

Karin Peterson

Kathy Zimmer   Wanda Coats   Cranston Davenport   Jill Sanders

Gallopade is proud to be a member of these educational organizations and associations:

Published by

GALLOPADE™ INTERNATIONAL

800-536-2GET
www.gallopade.com

SHOPA *MEMBER*™
School, Home, & Office Products Association

NSSEA

ASCD

The Illinois Experience Series

The Illinois Experience! Paperback Book

My First Pocket Guide to Illinois!

The Big Illinois Reproducible Activity Book

The Incredible Illinois Coloring Book!

My First Book About Illinois!

Illinois Jeopardy: Answers & Questions About Our State

Illinois "Jography!": A Fun Run Through Our State

The Illinois Experience! Sticker Pack

The Illinois Experience! Poster/Map

Discover Illinois CD-ROM

Illinois "GEO" Bingo Game

Illinois "HISTO" Bingo Game

A Word From The Author

Illinois is a very special state. Almost everything about Illinois is interesting and fun! It has a remarkable history that helped create the great nation of America. Illinois enjoys an amazing geography of incredible beauty and fascination. The state's people are unique and have accomplished many great things.

This Activity Book is chockful of activities to entice you to learn more about Illinois. While completing mazes, dot-to-dots, word searches, coloring activities, word codes, and other fun-to-do activities, you'll learn about Illinois's history, geography, people, places, animals, legends, and more.

Whether you're sitting in a classroom, stuck inside on a rainy day, or—better yet—sitting in the back seat of a car touring the wonderful state of Illinois, my hope is that you have as much fun using this Activity Book as I did writing it.

Enjoy your Illinois Experience—it's the trip of a lifetime!!

Carole Marsh

Fabulous Flag!

There are two dates on the Illinois flag. The first one, 1818, is when Illinois was admitted to the Union. The second, 1868, is when Illinois adopted its state seal.

ILLINOIS

What does the Illinois motto, *State Sovereignty, National Union mean?*

ANSWER: The Illinois motto means a democratic state that has allegiance to the unified nation.

Johnny's Apple Orchard

Johnny Appleseed wanted to plant apple trees and make America beautiful. As he traveled, he scattered apple seeds. Sometimes Johnny planted lots of apple trees together to make an orchard. He planted apple orchards in many states.

How many trees do you see in Johnny's apple orchard? **Write your answer here:**

Color the apple trees.

For extra fun, count the apples.
Write your answer here:

Johnny Appleseed's real name was John Chapman!

ANSWERS: 5 Trees, 35 Apples

In the Beginning. . . Came the French

In the late 1600s, René-Robert Cavelier, Sieur de La Salle of France followed the route of earlier French explorers and canoed down the Mississippi River. He established Fort Saint Louis at Starved Rock on the Illinois River and tried, unsuccessfully, to claim the entire Mississippi Basin for France.

Help Sieur de La Salle find his way to the fort.

Start

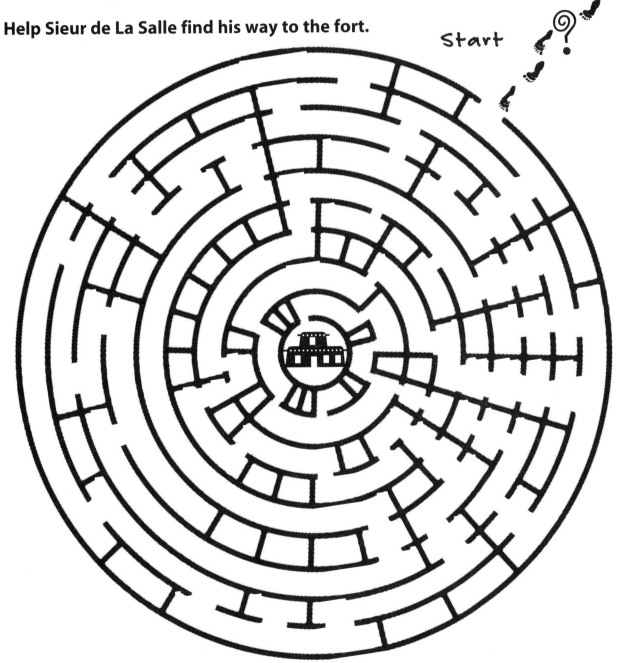

FRANTIC FISH

Word Search

Illinois has many rivers and lakes, mainly in the southern part of the state. Fishing is a popular activity in the rivers and lakes of Illinois.

Find the names of some fish that lurk in the waters of Illinois.

Did you know that most of Illinois' lakes are man-made and over 180 species of fish inhabit these waters?

BLUEGILL
BUFFALO FISH
BULLHEADS
CARP

CATFISH
CRAPPIE
PERCH
SALMON

SAUGERS
SMELT
SUNFISH
WALLEYE

```
B  U  L  L  H  E  A  D  S  Z  B  K
C  B  S  D  A  B  A  A  L  U  C  S
A  L  U  Q  R  O  U  V  F  H  B  A
R  U  N  E  W  G  L  F  S  P  T  L
P  E  F  T  E  G  A  I  S  E  F  M
F  G  I  R  K  L  F  P  A  R  X  O
M  I  S  K  O  T  O  L  I  C  S  N
D  L  H  F  A  E  P  B  S  H  G  R
E  L  I  C  R  A  P  P  I  E  A  O
D  S  M  E  L  T  H  R  D  N  O  L
H  W  A  L  L  E  Y  E  M  H  T  G
```

Buzzing Around Illinois!

Find the answers to the questions in the maze. Write them on the lines. Follow a path through the maze in the same order as your answers to get the bee to the beehive.

Illinois is bordered by the _____ River.

Illinois was the _____ state.

Illinois is in _____ America.

_____ were the first people to live in Illinois.

The _____ is a major river in Illinois.

Illinois is also called the _____ State.

The capital of Illinois is _____.

_____ was the 16th president of the United States.

The _____ Hills are in Southern Illinois.

The Indians that Illinois is named for are the _____.

_____ has its company headquarters in Moline.

ILLINOIS IMMIGRATION

Throughout its history, even when it was a territory, immigrants have been attracted to Illinois in search of a better life. People came from all over the world, and like the ocean, they came in waves. The American South provided the first settlers to Illinois. Interestingly enough, these southerners tended to settle in the southern part of the state of Illinois. The opening of the Erie Canal cleared the way for people to relocate from New England. The New Englanders primarily settled in the northern half of the state. By the 1830s, the state was divided between Yankees and Southerners.

The second wave of immigrants came from Europe in the 1840s. Immigration continued for 100 years. These people were from Germany, Sweden, China, India, Japan, Italy, Ireland, and many other countries.

The third wave took place in the early twentieth century when African-Americans moved up from the rural South. This was during the time that Illinois was becoming less agricultural and more industrial. People were in search of factory jobs.

Since the mid-1950s, the largest number of immigrants has come from Asia and Central and South America.

Use the rhyming clues to fill in the blanks.

1. People left their land of strife to come to Illinois for a better __ __ __ __ .

2. Wonderful people came and none could be finer than those that came from India and __ __ __ __ __ .

3. Immigrants are people who are very brave and those going to Illinois came in a __ __ __ __ .

4. The second wave came with smiles and tears and continued to immigrate for __ __ __ years.

5. The New Englanders arrived tired and weary and traveled through a canal by the name of __ __ __ __ .

6. The men came, all those Henrys and Bobs, and arrived in the city in search of new __ __ __ __ .

Answers: 1. life, 2. China, 3. wave, 4. 100, 5. Erie, 6. jobs.

Friend or Foe?

In the late 1600s, Father Jacques Marquette and Louis Jolliet sailed down the Mississippi River and encountered the friendly Illini Indians. The Indians helped the two Europeans by showing them a shortcut from the Mississippi River to Lake Michigan. With the help of the Indians, Marquette and Jolliet found the site of modern day Chicago.

Help the Indian reach the Europeans that are traveling by canoe down the Mississippi River.

The Illini Indians were actually a confederation of about 12 tribes which all spoke the same language, called Algonquin.

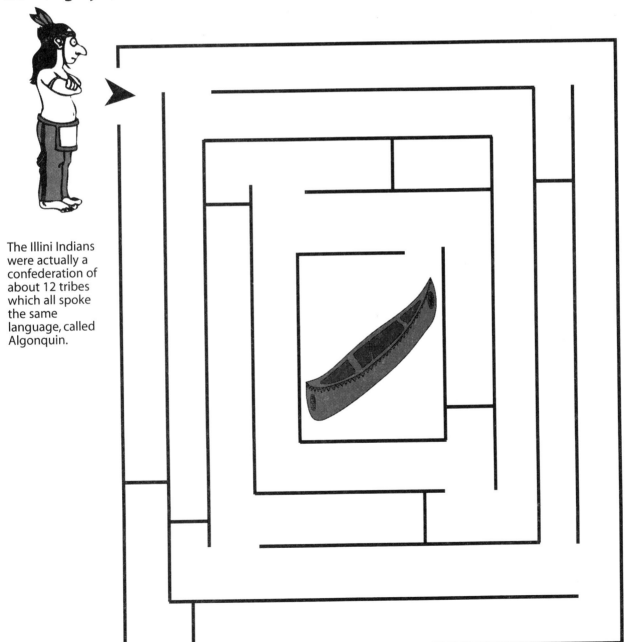

Rhymin' Riddles

I am a state in the Midwest and my name starts with an "I";
From all around, to see me, many do come by.

What am I? _____

I lived on the land of Illinois before the Iroquois did come;
Saplings covered with tree bark near a river was my home.

Who am I? _____

Up the Mississippi and through Lake Michigan,
With the help of the Illini Indians our journey did begin.

What am I? _____

I was from France, and down the Mississippi I did sail,
The land of Illinois I saw was sure to prevail.

Who am I? _____

Through the middle of Illinois is how I flow;
I begin in Chicago and all the cities in between I know.

What am I? _____

ANSWERS: Illinois, Illini Indian, Jolliet and Marquette, Sieur de La Salle, Illinois River

Illinois! Bubblegram

Bubble up on your knowledge of Illinois' bordering states and bodies of water.

Fill in the bubblegram by using the clues below.

1. A state south of Illinois
2. A body of water west of Illinois
3. A state east of Illinois
4. A state west of illinois
5. A river that is the southeast border of Illinois
6. A state southwest of Illinois
7. A body of water north of Illinois
8. A state east of Illinois and north of Indiana

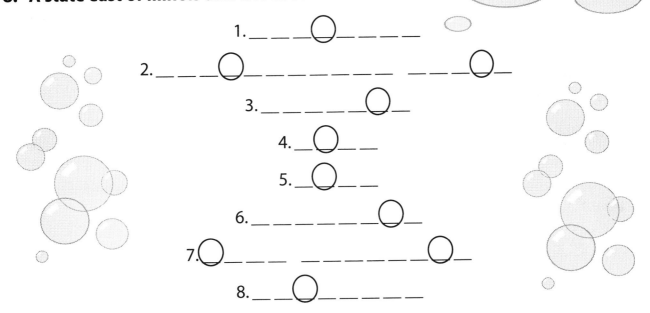

Now unscramble the "bubble" letters to discover the mystery word.

MYSTERY WORD: C _ _ _ L _ _ _ _ N

Hint: This town in Illinois has the largest statue of Abe Lincoln.

Famous Illinoisans

The most famous person that Ilinois is known for is Abraham Lincoln. He was the sixteenth president of the United States and he led the Union forces in the Civil War. He signed the Emancipation Proclamation in 1863 declaring freedom for all slaves in areas still under Confederate control. Ulysses S. Grant was another Illinoisan. He lived in Galena. He was the eighteenth president of the United States and a great Union general in the Civil War. Ernest Hemingway, a novelist, won the Nobel Prize in Literature in 1954 and was a native of our state. Gwendolyn Brooks, an Illinois poet, wrote passionately about the frustrations of African-Americans in America. She received the Pulitzer Prize for her work in 1950. John Deere introduced the steel plow in Illinois to cut through prairie sod. Now, with headquarters in Moline, the John Deere name is known worldwide. Did you know Walt Disney was born in Chicago? Of course you know he was a motion picture animator, producer, and creator of Disneyland and Disney World. George W.G. Ferris of Galesburg created the first Ferris Wheel. It was so big it could hold more than 2,000 people at once! Elijah P. Lovejoy was a famous newsman and abolitionist. He helped organize the Illinois Anti-Slavery Society. George M. Pullman improved and marketed the railway sleeping car. Former U.S. President Ronald Reagan is from Illinois. Upton Sinclair was a famous writer who uncovered the unsanitary conditions of meat-packing plants in Chicago.

Now fill in the blanks to name something significant about some of these famous people. Follow the example:

Abraham Lincoln	President of the U.S. and leader of the Union
Upton Sinclair	_____
Elijah P. Lovejoy	_____
George W.G. Ferris	_____
Walt Disney	_____
Ronald Reagan	_____
Ernest Hemingway	_____

Sing Like an Illinois Bird Word Jumble

Arrange the jumbled letters in the proper order for the names of birds found in Illinois.

BLUE JAY

CARDINAL

CROW

BLACKBIRD

QUAIL

WOODPECKER

PHEASANT

SPARROW

CHICKADEE

WARBLER

N I D L A R A C _ _ _ _ _ _ _ _

L D B I C K R A B _ _ _ _ _ _ _ _ _

U Q L A I _ _ _ _ _

R O W C _ _ _ _

S P R R W O A _ _ _ _ _ _ _

B E U L A J Y _ _ _ _ _ _ _

N T H P E A S A _ _ _ _ _ _ _ _

D O O W P C E E K R _ _ _ _ _ _ _ _ _ _

B R L W A R E _ _ _ _ _ _ _

H C I K D E A E C _ _ _ _ _ _ _ _ _

Our State Tree

The Illinois White Oak is the best known oak of all. The tree has a broad symmetrical crown and an overall majestic appearance. It has a light gray, scaly bark and the leaves have five to nine rounded lobes. Young leaves are pinkish or red, as are the leaves in Fall. The White Oak is an outstanding lumber tree, used for furniture, boats, and barrels.

Color the White Oak tree to show it in the Fall <u>or</u> Spring.

Gypsy moth larvae kill White Oaks by devouring their leaves.

Painted Turtle

Painted Turtles live in waterways all across North America, from the East Coast to the West Coast. Illinois is a haven for the painted turtle as well as others. The Illinois mud turtle and spotted turtle are on Illinois' endangered list.

"Paint" this turtle using the color key.

COLOR KEY

R = red   B = blue
Y = yellow G = green

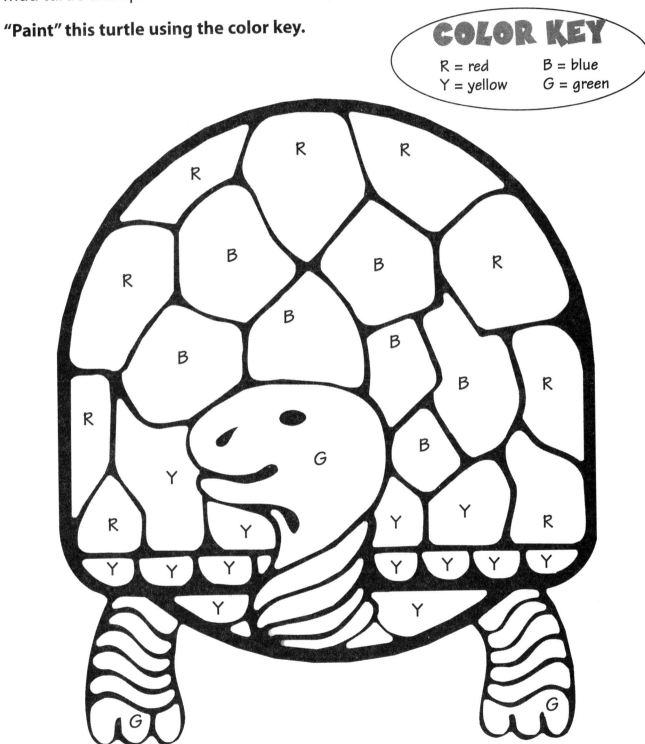

How many spots are on this turtle? _____

Make a Wampum Necklace!

Illinois Indians used wampum (beads made from colored shells) to barter with early settlers. They traded wampum for food and supplies. The Indians sometimes traded wampum for trinkets.

You can make your own wampum necklace using dried macaroni and string.
Thread the dried macaroni onto a long piece of string and tie.
Wear your necklace to show your pride in your state's heritage!

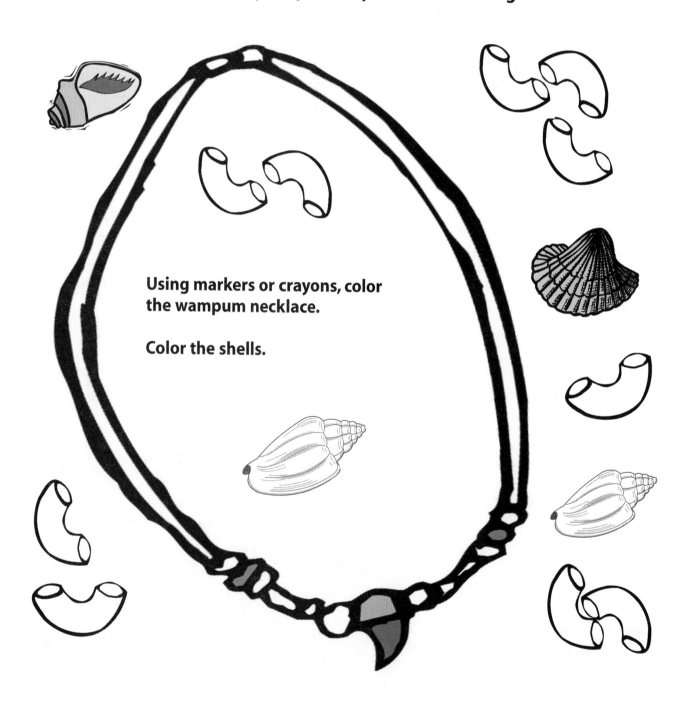

Using markers or crayons, color the wampum necklace.

Color the shells.

ILLINOIS WOMEN AND THE VOTE!

Women could not vote in Illinois until 1891. After that, they were only allowed to vote in school elections. In 1913, things began to change for women in Illinois. Our state became the first state east of the Mississippi River to pass a law allowing women to vote in a presidential election. In fact, in the 1916 presidential election 200,000 Illinois women showed up to vote! Now that's a good turnout for beginning voters! In 1919, the Illinois General Assembly ratified the Nineteenth Amendment to the United States Constitution. The following year the amendment became the law of the land and gave women throughout the United States the right to vote. Women today continue to be a major force in the election process.

Beside each item in Column A, write the number of the corresponding description in Column B.

A	B
_____ Amendment	1. It winds down Illinois' western edge and is the longest one in the nation
_____ Ratify	2. A law that is an acceptable practice throughout the nation
_____ Constitution	3. People who had no vote until 1913
_____ General Assembly	4. An addition to the Constitution
_____ Law of the Land	5. The selection, by vote, of a candidate for office
_____ Election	6. To give approval
_____ Mississippi River	7. The fundamental law of the United States that was framed in 1787 and put into effect in 1789
_____ Women	8. The legislature in some states of the United States

Answers: 1.4 2.6 3.7 4.8 5.2 6.5 7.1 8.3

Hull House

In the late 1800s, situations were tough for many immigrants, women, and children. Jane Addams and Ellen Gates Starr wanted to change conditions for these unfortunate people. They built what is known as the Hull House in Chicago as a haven for poor immigrants, women, and children. This was the beginning of social work in America. In 1931, Jane Addams was the first American woman awarded the Nobel Peace Prize.

Below is a description of a poor immigrant family. Pretend you are a helper in the Hull House. What would you do to help the family?

The year is 1925. The family is from Poland, and they had a very difficult time just getting through the immigration process at Ellis Island. Now they have decided to move to Chicago in search of factory jobs. They live in the slums, and the children cannot go to school because they have to work in the factories to make money for the family. The mother recently had a baby which is now 6 months old, and the other 3 children are ages 3, 6, and 11. The mom and dad cannot find babysitters for the two small children, and they are sad that their older children have to work long hours in the dangerous factories of Chicago.

How I could help:

_____

_____

_____

_____

_____

_____

_____

Althea lives at the Hull House. She is eager to welcome each new immigrant that arrives.

A Day in the Life of
an Illinois Settler!

Pretend you were a settler in the days of early Illinois.
You kept a diary of what you did each day.
Write in the "diary" what you might have done on a summer day in July, 1844.

_____

_____

_____

_____

_____

_____

_____

_____

_____

_____

_____

Illinois, The Prairie State!

Match the name of each Illinois state symbol on the left with its picture on the right.

Nickname

State Bird

State Animal

State Insect

State Flower

State Tree

State Fish

State Fossil

The Prairie State

Illinois kids voted for the state tree and state flower!

The First Americans

When European explorers first arrived in America, they found many American Indian tribes living here.

Illinois Indians lived in the Eastern Woodland region of the United States. The types of homes they lived in were wigwams.
Color the Eastern Woodland green.

Plains Indians lived all over the Great Plains region of North America. Some Plains Indians lived in teepees.
Color the Great Plains yellow.

Pueblo Indians lived in the Southwest region of North America. They lived in multi-story terraced buildings, called pueblos. **Color the Southwest red.**

Color these Indian houses.
Draw a line from the type of house to the correct region.

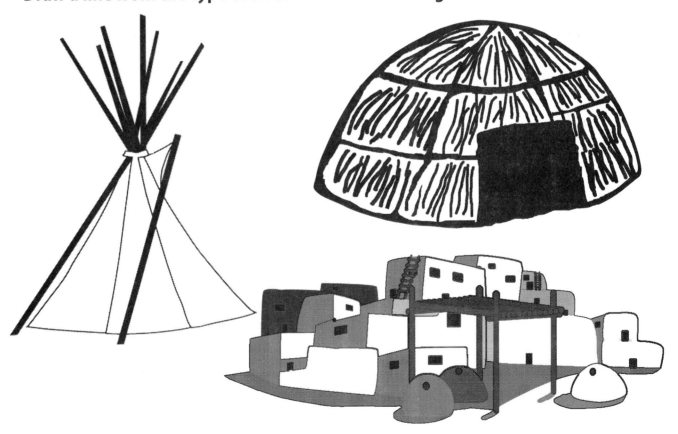

The First Ferris Wheel

The original Ferris Wheel was built in Chicago for the 1893 World's Fair Exposition. It was built by, and named for, George W.G. Ferris of Galesburg. The wheel was so huge that two thousand people could ride on it at once! In fact, it was 250 feet (76 meters) high. Today, Ferris Wheels are popular at carnivals, amusement parks, and fairs. Usually they are much smaller, about 50 feet (15 meters) in diameter, and can be erected in a few hours by a small crew of workmen. They can be quickly dismantled.

Brain Busters:

1. If 2,000 people are riding the Ferris Wheel on one ride, how many people will ride it on ten rides? _____

2. If only half the people ride on one ride, how many people will be riding? _____

3. If the first Ferris Wheel was 250 feet tall, how many yards was that? _____

4. The new Ferris Wheels are _____ the size of the original. (Use fractions)

5. How many years before the end of the nineteenth century was the Ferris Wheel built? _____

6. If the Ferris Wheel was invented in 1893, how old will it be in the year 2020? _____

Color the Ferris Wheel.

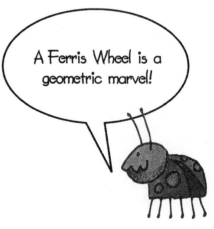

A Ferris Wheel is a geometric marvel!

ILLINOIS SPELLING BEE

Good spelling is a good habit. Study the words on the left side of the page. Then fold the page in half and "take a spelling test" on the right side. Have a buddy read the words aloud to you. When done, unfold the page and check your spelling. Keep your score. GOOD LUCK.

ombudsman	1. _____
architecture	2. _____
Bloomington	3. _____
Black Hawk	4. _____
constitution	5. _____
Wabash	6. _____
zeppelin	7. _____
yesteryear	8. _____
Jurassic	9. _____
Kishwaukee	10. _____
Marquette	11. _____
obelisk	12. _____
Shawneetown	13. _____
unemployment	14. _____
general assembly	15. _____

Each of the 15 items is worth 5 points. 75 is a perfect score. How many did you get right?

Disco Polly Gets A Plow

Polly lives in a little farming town in Illinois named Disco. She helps her father grow corn and soybeans. Today is a very special day for Polly. She is going to Grand Detour with her family to buy a John Deere plow for the farm. John Deere plows are a new invention that make work on the farm much easier.

Help Polly find her way to Grand Detour.

Beautiful Butterfly!

Using the key, color the picture of Illinois' state insect.

COLOR KEY:

1. black   2. yellow   3. orange   4. gray

Write the name of this lovely insect in the space provided.

_____ _____ Butterfly

Independence Day

We celebrate America's birthday on July 4. We call the 4th of July Independence Day because this is the day America declared its independence from England.

Circle the things you might enjoy on this special holiday.

Pretend you are signing the Declaration of Independence.

Write your signature here.

You can make it fancy!

Declaration of Independence

_____

What in the World?

A hemisphere is one-half of a sphere (globe) created by the prime meridian or equator. Every place in the world is in two hemispheres (Northern or Southern and Eastern or Western). The equator is an imaginary line that runs around the world from left to right and divides the globe into the Northern Hemisphere and Southern Hemisphere. Illinois is in the Northern Hemisphere.

The prime meridian is an imaginary line that runs around the world from top to bottom and divides the globe into the Eastern Hemisphere and Western Hemisphere. Illinois is in the Western Hemisphere.

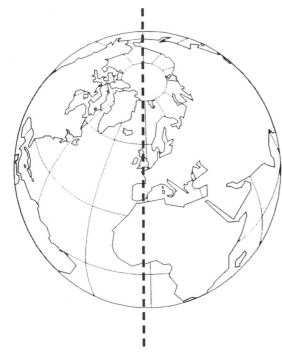

Label the Eastern and Western Hemispheres.

Write PM on the prime meridian.

Color the map.

Label the Northern and Southern Hemispheres.

Write E on the equator.

Color the map.

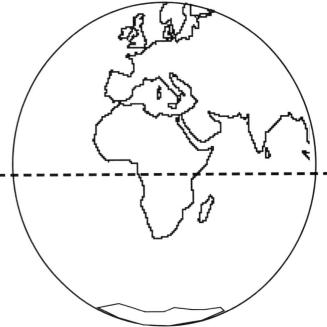

Color Me!

ILLINOIS

Brown
Like the hickory tree.
Brown

BLUE
Like the Illinois sky.
Blue

YELLOW
Like fresh corn.
Yellow

RED
Like the Cardinal!
Red

BLACK
Like the stripes
on a honeybee.
Black

PURPLE
Like the Illinois native Violet.
Purple

GREEN
Like the prairies.
Green

ORANGE
Like a pumpkin.
Orange

Key to a Map!

A map key, also called a map legend, shows symbols which represent different things on a map.

Match each word with a symbol for things found in the state of Illinois.

Airport

Church

Historic Site

Railroad

River

Road

School

State Capital

Civil War Museum

Bird Sanctuary

Pirates? In Illinois?!

Yes, Illinois had its fair share of pirates! Where did they come from? Illinois does have rivers, and many pirates preyed on pioneer families on the Illinois River in Southern Illinois. A favorite pirate hideout was Cave-in-Rock, which was a cavern on the Illinois River. The pirates would lure thirsty travelers in with signs that promised "liquor vault and house of entertainment." There have been no river pirates in more than a century.

Color the Treasure Chest.
Woodgrain=brown,
Trim=yellow,
Round Jewels=blue and green.
Add all the booty (treasure) inside you want!

Something Fishy Here!

Want to see the world's largest indoor collection of fish and other sea creatures? Just head to the John G. Shedd Aquarium in Chicago! Here, visitors can view a vast collection of brightly colored fish, sharks, turtles, and many more varieties of sea creatures. You can even watch a diver feed the fish and turtles in the giant tank at the center of the aquarium. Speaking of fish…

Draw what you might see in the waters of the giant tank on a visit to the John G. Shedd Aquarium.

What Did They Eateth?
Early American Food Trivia

Below are some foods that Illinoisans ate long ago.
Some are still eaten today, but not named the same!

Match the food with its definition.

1. Scrambled eggs and brains _____
2. Apple pancakes _____
3. Hominy _____
4. Horseshoe sandwich _____
5. Chicago style hot dog _____
6. Porterhouse steak _____
7. Sauerkraut _____
8. Rhubarb Cream pie _____
9. Weiner Schnitzel _____
10. Blood sausage _____
11. Scrapple _____
12. Sweet tomato pickles _____

A. A unique T-Bone
B. Sausage made with pork blood
C. Sour pickled cabbage
D. Soft corn dish
E. Cereal sausage dish
F. Tomatoes cooked and preserved in vinegar
G. Hot dog with special toppings
H. Sandwich made with French fries & cheese sauce
I. German dish made with pounded veal
J. Eggs made with pork brains
K. Pancakes baked with apples
L. Fruit in a thick custard

How many did you get right?

Are you hungry now?

Let's eateth!

ALL AROUND ILLINOIS

Illinois is bordered by five different states. These states are called neighboring states. We also have a very large lake as part of our northeastern border. To learn where we are located in the United States, it helps to know our neighbors.

On the map below, write the names of our neighboring states, then color them yellow. Name the one lake that borders our state. Color it blue. Color Illinois red.

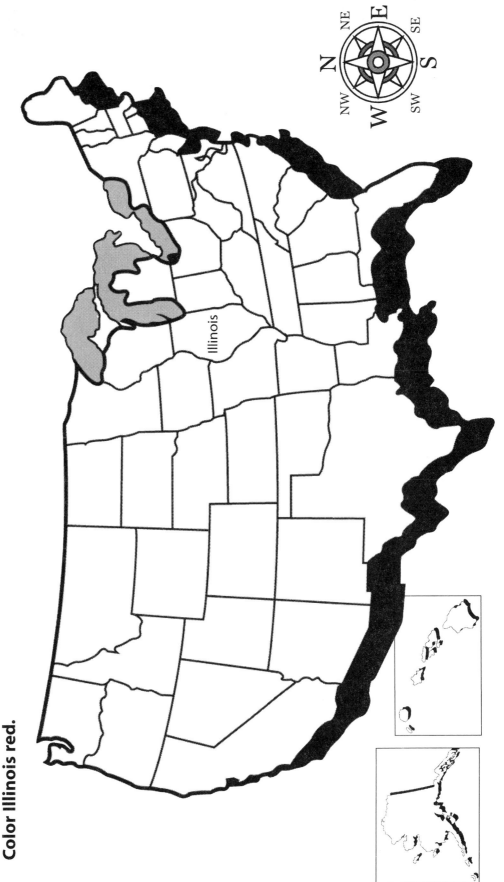

Illinois

Yes, Susie, There Was a Settler's Christmas!

An early Christmas custom in olden-day Illinois was to create a "goodie string" filled with treats. The "goodie string" was hung from the door, and each young visitor was allowed to choose a Christmas treat, such as candy, nuts, fruit, or small toys.

Draw your own "goodie string" of Christmas delights.
When you finish, color it in Christmas colors.

Map of North America

This is a map of North America. Illinois is one of the 50 states in North America.

Color the state of Illinois red.

Color the rest of the United States yellow. Alaska and Hawaii are part of the United States and should also be colored yellow.

Color Canada green. Color Mexico blue.

Symbols of the United States

These are some of the symbols that remind us of America. These symbols are honored and respected in our country.

Color each symbol.

American Flag

Statue of Liberty

Bald Eagle

Liberty Bell

Home Sweet Home

Match these famous Illinois authors with their native or adopted hometowns. One city is the hometown of three authors. Use that letter three times.

A = Chicago; B = Lewistown; C = Peoria; D = Galesburg; E = Waukegan; F = Oak Park

_____ 1. Carl Sandburg: poet who also wrote *Abraham Lincoln: The Prairie Years*

_____ 2. Ernest Hemingway: author of the novel, *The Old Man and the Sea*

_____ 3. Lorraine Hansberry: playwright who wrote *A Raisin in the Sun*

_____ 4. Gwendolyn Brooks: named the poet laureate of Illinois in 1968

_____ 5. Edgar Lee Masters: wrote *The Spoon River Anthology*

_____ 6. Saul Bellow: winner of Nobel Prize for literature

_____ 7. Ray Bradbury: writer of science fiction, *The Martian Chronicles*

_____ 8. Betty Friedan: activist and author of *The Feminine Mystique*

ANSWERS: 1-D, 2-F, 3-A, 4-A, 5-B, 6-A, 7-E, 8-C

Illinois Cities

Circle Springfield in red. It is our state's capital. The star is the map symbol for our capital.

Circle Peoria in yellow. It is the third largest city in Illinois.

Circle East St. Louis in blue. It is the eastern half of the city of St. Louis, Missouri.

Circle Chicago in brown. It is the largest, busiest city in Illinois.

Circle Champaign-Urbana in orange. It is the home of the renowned University of Illinois.

Add your city or town to the map if it's not here. Circle it in green. Give it a 🙂 symbol to show you live there.

Oops! The compass rose is missing its cardinal directions.

Write N, S, E, W, on the compass rose.

The Bald Eagle Riddle

The bald eagle is a national symbol of the United States. It appears on the state flag and the state symbol of Illinois.

Read the riddle and name each part of the Bald Eagle using words from the Word Bank.

I keep the eagle warm and dry. I am brown on the eagle's body and wings. I am white on the eagle's head and tail.
What am I?_____

I help the eagle stand and wade in shallow water to catch fish as they swim past.
What am I?_____

I am the eagle's home. Sometimes I measure 12 feet across.
What am I?_____

I help the eagle fly high into the sky. I measure 7 to 8 feet across.
What am I? _____

I am yellow. I help the eagle catch and eat fish.
What am I?_____

WORD BANK

nest   wings   bill
feet   feathers

ANSWERS: feathers, feet, nest, wings, bill

Illinois Haystacks

Illinois is one of the nation's largest producers of farm machinery. It was here that John Deere invented a plow in 1837 that made it possible to farm the prairie. His plow broke the soil better than earlier plows did. Its sharp blades cut through tangled roots. Deere's invention revolutionized farming practices in the nineteenth century. The headquarters of the John Deere Company is now in Moline. Moline is also known as the Farm Implement Capital of the World. Illinois is known for its agriculture and produces such crops as corn, soybeans, and wheat. When driving through Illinois, you may see many haystacks in the fields. Read below about how to make your own "haystacks"!

You will need:

1 - 8 oz. jar of peanut butter

1 - 12 oz. bag of butterscotch morsels

1 - 16 oz. can of chow mein noodles

Step 1.   Melt peanut butter together with butterscotch morsels.

Step 2.   Add chow mein noodles.

Step 3.   Drop by spoonfuls on cookie sheet and chill.

Step 4.   Enjoy!

Meet Joe Black

Joe Black is a coal miner in southern Illinois. He is strong. He works hard. His father and grandfather worked in the coal mines. He is saving his money so his kids can go to college.

Joe uses many tools in his job: a pick, a shovel, and a canary. A canary? That's right! He lowers it down into the mine to be sure there are no toxic fumes that would be harmful to the miners.

Help Joe Black pull the canary safely from the mine!

FINISH

START

Good Golly! Geography Word Search

See if you can find the Illinois cities in the Word Search.

ALLEGHENY

SPRINGFIELD

JOLIET

DIXON

ROCK ISLAND

PRAIRIE

CHICAGO

PEORIA

EVANSTON

QUINCY

ILLINOIS

CHAMPAIGN

BLOOMINGTON

MOLINE

DECATUR

LINCOLN

```
B F A C J O L I E T R
L S L P R A I R I E R
O P L K B L N B S T N
O R E U M N C V I A R
M I G H S T O V K N D
I N H M U R L S U T C
N G E Q U I N C Y S P
G F N R O C K B U O E
T I Y O C H I C A G O
O E T A D E C A T U R
N L I E I A S M K V I
T D N O X U S B R I A
I S T M O L I N E K M
R E V A N S T O N U V
V R O C K I S L A N D
S C H A M P A I G N S
C I L L I N O I S U B
```

Welcome to the Land of Lincoln!

This Old House!

Take yourself back 100 years. Can you imagine what life would be like in the Victorian Era? What did turn-of-the-century Illinoisans have? How did they live? See if you can pick out which of the following items people at the turn of the century had and which ones they did not.

Circle the things you find or use around your 1900 home.

The First Thanksgiving

Help the pioneers prepare a Thanksgiving. The first people of Illinois couldn't possibly forget to celebrate Thanksgiving.

Draw a circle around each type of food from the Word Bank hidden in the picture.

Then color the picture.

WORD BANK

corn	pumpkin	carrots
squash	turkey	apples
onion	beans	pear
cherries	fish	potato

Illinois Rules!

Use the code to complete the sentences.

A B C D E F G H I J K L M N O P Q R S T
1 2 3 4 5 6 7 8 9 10 11 12 13 14 15 16 17 18 19 20

U V W X Y Z
21 22 23 24 25 26

1. State rules are called ___ ___ ___ ___.
                              12 1 23 19

2. Laws are made in Springfield at our state ___ ___ ___ ___ ___ ___ ___.
                                                        3 1 16 9 20 15 12

3. The leader of our state is the ___ ___ ___ ___ ___ ___ ___ ___.
                                  7 15 22 5 18 14 15 18

4. We live in the state of ___ ___ ___ ___ ___ ___ ___ ___.
                          9 12 12 9 14 15 9 19

5. The capital of our state is ___ ___ ___ ___ ___ ___ ___ ___ ___ ___ ___.
                         19 16 18 9 14 7 6 9 5 12 4

Who Am I?

Can you figure out who these famous Illinoisans are? Use the Word Bank to help you.

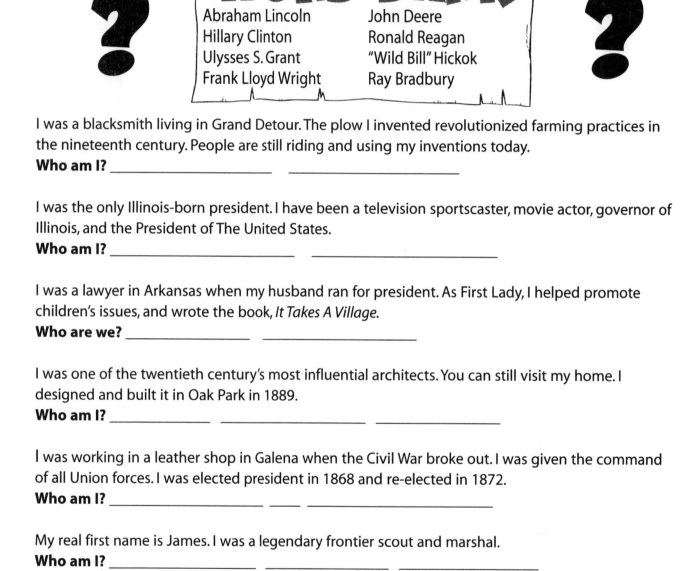

WORD BANK

Abraham Lincoln   John Deere
Hillary Clinton   Ronald Reagan
Ulysses S. Grant   "Wild Bill" Hickok
Frank Lloyd Wright   Ray Bradbury

I was a blacksmith living in Grand Detour. The plow I invented revolutionized farming practices in the nineteenth century. People are still riding and using my inventions today.
Who am I? _____ _____

I was the only Illinois-born president. I have been a television sportscaster, movie actor, governor of Illinois, and the President of The United States.
Who am I? _____ _____

I was a lawyer in Arkansas when my husband ran for president. As First Lady, I helped promote children's issues, and wrote the book, *It Takes A Village*.
Who are we? _____ _____

I was one of the twentieth century's most influential architects. You can still visit my home. I designed and built it in Oak Park in 1889.
Who am I? _____ _____ _____

I was working in a leather shop in Galena when the Civil War broke out. I was given the command of all Union forces. I was elected president in 1868 and re-elected in 1872.
Who am I? _____ _____ _____

My real first name is James. I was a legendary frontier scout and marshal.
Who am I? _____ _____ _____

FLASH BACK!

TAKE YOURSELF BACK IN TIME......

The time is March 6, 1857. You find yourself sitting in the back of an old-time courtroom. Standing in the front of the room is a Missouri slave named Dred Scott who was brought by his master, John Emerson, to Illinois. Mr. Emerson died a few years back and Dred Scott is seeking freedom. The argument is that Illinois is a free state and Wisconsin, where he moved from with his master, is a free state. Therefore, Scott should be a free man. However, as you watch the drama unfold before you, the courts hand down the decision that Dred Scott is still ruled to be a slave. The impact of the ruling will go far beyond this courtroom. Even though the audience here cannot see into the future, tensions and emotions run high. Another aspect of the ruling that has been handed down is that Congress has no power to exclude slavery from territories. It also declares that blacks cannot be citizens. You watch as outraged opponents of slavery create havoc with their yelling and anger.
Pay careful attention to what you are watching. It is these tensions that will lead to the Civil War.

NOW DUST YOURSELF OFF AND COME BACK TO THE FUTURE!
ISN'T IT GOOD TO BE HOME?

MATCH THE FOLLOWING:

1. What was the name of the main player in this court case? _____ _____

2. What was the master's name? _____ _____

3. The ruling was that _____ has no power to exclude slavery from territories.

4. In what century was this famous trial taking place? _____

5. These unfortunate decisions came during a cold season. What was it?_____

6. This ruling and other tensions led to what event?_____ _____

7. Where was the Dred Scott decision handed down? _____

8. What 2 free states did Dred Scott live in? _____ _____

9. Did the impact of this ruling stay within this case? _____ yes _____ no

10. What was the emotional climate of the courtroom? _____

Answers: 1. Dred Scott, 2. John Emerson, 3. Congress, 4. Nineteenth, 5. Winter, 6. Civil War, 7. Illinois, 8. Illinois, Wisconsin, 9. No 10. Tense, angry

Illinois, The Great Prairie

The Illinois prairie is very special. Millions of years ago it was formed by glaciers that traveled across the landscape making it flat. At first, people were disappointed with the flat, useless land, but Illinois has some of the richest soil in America.

How many of each plant or animal can you find in this old schoolhouse scene? Write your answers below.

How many?

An Illinois Harvest

Match the name of each crop or product from Illinois with the picture of that item.

apples   tomatoes   watermelon   pumpkin   corn

Move to the Big City

You have lived in Erie, a small Illinois town, all your life. Your family has made the decision to move to a big city. What will you do? Where will you live? How will you get around? You write a letter to your Chicago friend and ask her all these questions. This is what she writes back to you:

Dear

_____

_____

_____

_____

_____

_____

_____

_____

_____

_____

Bird Search!

Find the names of these birds commonly found in Illinois in the word search below.

HERON   ROBIN   BLUE JAY   CARDINAL
WOOD DUCK   HUMMINGBIRD   MALLARD   CHICKADEE
TEAL   CROW   HAWK   FINCH   KILLDEER

```
F  R  C  B  H  I  L  M  Y  W  Q  O  C  I  P
H  T  F  A  X  M  R  Q  W  O  I  U  A  X  O
G  H  I  R  O  B  I  N  C  M  V  E  R  W  Q
X  Z  N  T  S  L  R  O  H  E  W  Q  D  J  Y
S  Q  C  G  H  U  M  M  I  N  G  B  I  R  D
F  X  H  R  E  E  O  B  C  A  Q  X  N  T  Y
S  C  H  R  O  J  E  W  K  B  V  M  A  K  O
W  R  O  Z  X  A  O  U  A  B  P  L  I  X
Q  O  V  M  E  Y  I  H  D  P  R  T  M  L  V
E  W  O  V  A  P  E  R  E  P  T  E  A  L  M
S  Q  P  D  M  L  P  M  E  R  P  B  M  D  Z
F  R  W  Q  D  M  L  V  C  N  O  V  P  E  X
C  V  B  N  O  U  Z  A  O  E  V  N  O  E  M
V  C  Z  O  E  H  C  O  R  M  O  Z  T  R  O
T  Y  E  Q  H  A  W  K  V  D  O  T  M  X  Y
```

Illinois' Venomous Snakes!

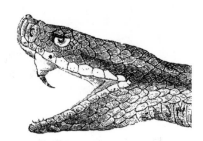

Below are three species of venomous (poisonous) snakes that live in Illinois.
Using the alphabet code, see if you can find out their names.

Use the code to complete the sentences.

A	B	C	D	E	F	G	H	I	J	K	L	M	N	O	P	Q	R	S	T
1	2	3	4	5	6	7	8	9	10	11	12	13	14	15	16	17	18	19	20

U	V	W	X	Y	Z
21	22	23	24	25	26

_____

5 1 19 20 5 18 14   3 15 20 20 15 14 13 15 21 20 8

14 15 18 20 8 5 18 14   3 15 16 16 5 18 8 5 1 4

20 9 13 2 5 18   18 1 20 20 12 5 19 14 1 11 5

Crossroads Illinois!

One of the most important things about the state of Illinois is its strategic location.
Check the following that are true about the state:

_____ Located in the heart of the United States
_____ Located at the junction of key water routes
_____ Links the eastern U.S. with the west
_____ Links the Great Lakes with the Gulf of Mexico
_____ Links America's heartland with foreign markets

Now, answer the following questions about Illinois' strategic geographic location.

1. Illinois is bounded by three rivers, the _____, _____, and the _____.

2. _____ _____ connects the St. Lawrence Seaway to the Atlantic Ocean.

3. Three types of transportation that link Chicago to many other places are: _____ , _____ and _____.

4. Because Illinois goods have so many ways to travel around the world, the state is a leading _____:
   a. importer
   b. exporter
   c. travel agent

5. Illinois has more than 130,000 miles (209,215 kilometers) of these:
   a. railroad track
   b. roads and highways
   c. roller coasters

Chicago's O'Hare International Airport is one of the busiest in the world!

4.b, 5.b

ANSWERS: All are true. 1. Ohio, Wabash, Mississippi. 2. Lake Michigan. 3. air, rail, and ships.

Getting Ready To Vote

When you turn 18, you will be eligible to vote. Your vote counts! Many elections have been won by just a few votes. The following is a form for your personal voting information. You will need to be a good research student to get all the answers!

I will be eligible to vote on this date _____

I live in this Congressional District   _____

I live in this State Senate District _____

I live in this State Representative District _____

I live in this Voting Precinct _____

The first local election I can vote in will be _____

The first state election I can vote in will be _____

The first national election I can vote in will be _____

The governor of our state is _____

One of my state senators is _____

One of my state representatives is _____

The local public office I would like to run for is _____

The state public office I would like to run for is _____

The federal public office I would like to run for is _____

Did you know our state has 59 senators?

No, but I do know we have 118 state representatives!

Illinois In The Civil War

Illinois was heavily involved in the Civil War. About 15% of Illinois' population actively participated in the war, giving it the second highest percentage of citizens going to war of any state. Although Illinois was devoted to the Union cause, many sections of southern Illinois stayed in touch with Confederate officials and encouraged Union soldiers to desert. These traitors were known as Copperheads because of their snake-like, sneaky behavior.

Pretend you are a citizen of Illinois during the Civil War. Keep in mind that Abraham Lincoln, from Illinois, is the President of the Union. Which side would you fight for? Remember the reasons for war (slavery and state's rights) and the various problems that brought on the war. Write down your thoughts below.

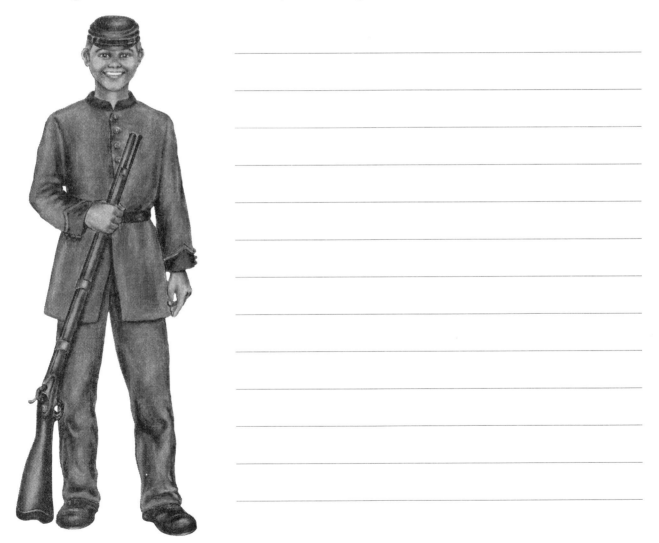

Illinois Law Comes In Many Flavors!

Here is a matching activity for you to see just a few of the many kinds of laws it takes to run our state. See how well you do!

If I am this,
I might use what type of law?

1. Bank robber
2. Business person
3. State park
4. Illinois
5. Hospital
6. Real estate agent
7. Corporation
8. Ship owner
9. Diplomat
10. Soldier

Laws of many types

A. Military Law
B. International Law
C. Constitutional Law
D. Medical Law
E. Maritime Law
F. Commercial Law
G. Criminal Law
H. Property Law
I. Antitrust Law
J. Environmental Law

Illinois Word Search

Find the words from the Word Bank in the puzzle below.

WORD BANK

SETTLER
CHICAGO
DU SABLE
LINCOLN
INDIANS
FUR TRADE
GRANT
BARTER

SANDBURG
ADDAMS
JOLLIET
MARQUETTE
KASKASKIA
LA SALLE
STARVED ROCK

```
F D U S A B L E M R H
U T B E C C K L A V U
R K E T L H F I R D L
T S Q T L I K N Q S L
R T L L N C B D U K H
A H V E S A V I E D O
D M I R A G U A T L S
E H K Q N O I N T I S
R T A D D A M S E N E
A J S R B L B O C C L
Y O K B U A T E R O A
O L A A R S R B A L N
K L S R G A G R A N T
S I K T R L C D T N G
B E I E S L S N O A T
S T A R V E D R O C K
```

A River Runs Through It!

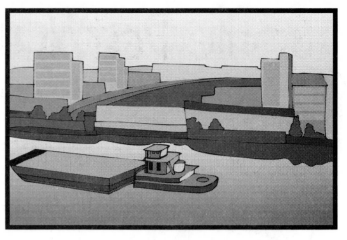

The state of Illinois is blessed with many rivers. See if you can wade right in and figure out which river name completes the sentences below!

1. If you make a mistake and blush, you might find yourself wanting to duck and hide in the __ __ __ __ __ __ __ __ __ River!

2. If you had a knife and a spoon, you could fix breakfast beside __ __ __ __ __ __ __ Fork.

3. Guess what? Here's a "utensil" Illinois River—it's the __ __ __ __ __ River!

4. Wipe your feet after you play in the __ __ __ __ __ River!

5. If you're looking for a "solution," check out the __ __ __ __ __ __ River.

6, You might need pepper, but not this at the __ __ __ __ River.

7. Wear a raincoat while playing in the __ __ __ __ __ __ __ __ River!

8. If you "kan" think about it, I'll bet you "kan" name this "kan" Illinois River, the __ __ __ __ __ __ __ __ .

9. When this river freezes in the winter, it's as hard as its name, the __ __ __ __ River.

10. The Green River is the opposite of the colorful name of the __ __ __ __ __ __ __ __ __ River!

Some Patriotic Holidays

FLAG DAY

Flag Day is celebrated on June 14 to honor our flag. Our country's flag is an important symbol. It makes us proud of our country. It makes us proud to be Americans.

Count the number of stars and stripes on the flag.

_____ Stars   _____ Stripes

MEMORIAL DAY

Memorial Day is also known as Decoration Day. We remember the people who died in wars and fought so that we could be free.

Circle the things you might put on a grave on Memorial Day.

VETERANS DAY

On Veterans Day we recognize Americans who served in the armed forces.

Circle ways we celebrate Veterans Day.

Getting There From Here!

Methods of transportation have changed in Illinois from the days of early explorers and the time when pioneers arrived and found Native Americans already living in Illinois.

Match each person to the way they would travel.

Native American

race car driver

child

settlers

astronaut

early explorer

pilot

Design your own Diamante on Illinois!

A *diamante* is a cool diamond-shaped poem on any subject. You can write your very own diamante poem on Illinois below by following the simple line by line directions. Give it a try!

Line 1: Write the name of your state.

Line 2: Write the names of two animals native to your state.

Line 3: Write the names of three of your state's important cities.

Line 4: Write the names of four of your state's important industries or agricultural products.

Line 5: Write the names of your state bird, the state flower, and state tree.

Line 6: Write the names of two of your state's geographical features.

Line 7: Write one word to describe your state.

_____

_____ _____

_____ _____ _____

_____ _____ _____ _____

_____ _____ _____

_____ _____

_____

Gwendolyn Brooks was named the poet laureate of Illinois in 1968. That means that she is Illinois' greatest living poet.

Illinois Word Wheel

From the Word Wheel of Illinois names, answer the following questions.

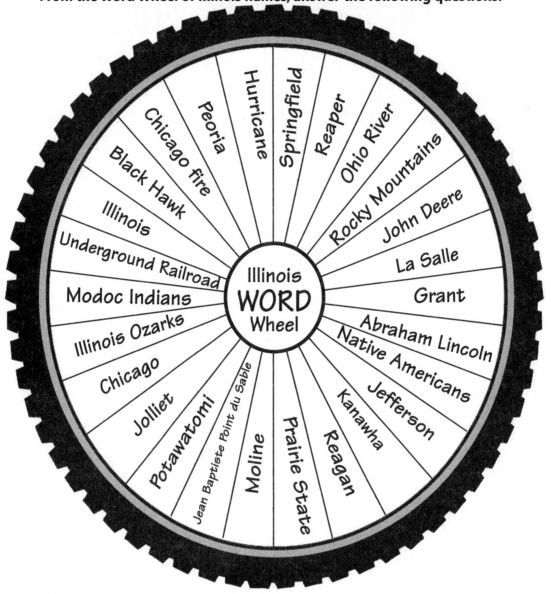

1. A famous president from Illinois who led the Union in the Civil War _____.
2. A French explorer who found Illinois with his partner_____.
3. The first people to live in Illinois were _____.
4. Illinois' nickname is the _____.
5. The great disaster that happened in 1871 was the _____ .
6. _____ introduced the first steel plow to cut through the prairie sod.
7. Cyrus McCormick invented the _____.
8. _____ is regarded as the founder of Chicago.
9. The Sauk Indians led by _____ were eventually defeated by the United States militia.
10. The Shawnee Hills are also referred to as the _____.

ANSWERS: 1. Abraham Lincoln, 2. Jolliet, 3. Modoc Indians, 4. Prairie State, 5. Chicago Fire, 6. John Deere, 7. reaper, 8. Jean Baptiste Point du Sable, 9. Black Hawk, 10. Illinois Ozarks

Rhymin' Riddles

In a one-room log cabin I began life; as I grew older, I saw lots of strife;
Slavery was wrong and I wanted none in the nation; as the 16th President, I signed
the Emancipation Proclamation.

Who am I? _____ _____

A pioneer and a trader were my occupations at first; I built the first home in Illinois dirt.
I am known as the founder of Chicago.

Who am I? _____ _____ _____ ___ _____ .

As an explorer many places I loved to see; Illinois was exciting for me.
My expedition saw many Indians, and to preach my religion, I was free.

Who am I? _____ _____

As an explorer on the Mississippi I built a fort and took my chance; for this
adventure I paid my dues and left my country and home in France.

Who am I? _____ ____ ___ _____

In 1983 I made history, the first African-American mayor of Chicago I became;
I was good to my people and enjoyed my fame.

Who am I? _____ _____

Early Native Americans Abound!

The first people ever to reach the land that would one day become the state of Illinois may have traveled across a frozen bridge of land linking Asia to North America. This continent to continent walk may have taken place as long as 30,000 years ago!

After they reached Illinois, Native Americans continued to travel and improve their way of life.

Can you complete the matching activity below?

1. Modoc Rock Shelter

2. wandering hunters

3. They traveled on foot because they had no ...

4. village homes

5. crops grown

6. seashells, copper, and minerals

7. used for religious ceremonies and burial

8. abandoned by 1500

A. Cahokia Mounds

B. corn and squash

C. nomads

D. trading tools

E. earthen mounds

F. horses

G. home to first Illinois inhabitants

H. domed houses of wood, grass, mud, and animal skins

Would you like to work on an archaeological dig?

Answers: 1.G, 2.C, 3.F, 4.H, 5.B, 6.D, 7.E, 8.A

What Shall I Be When I Grow Up?

Here are just a few of the jobs that kept early Illinoisans busy.

Lawyer	Farmer	Woodcarver
Judge	Housekeeper	Silversmith
Blacksmith	Dairyman	Wheelwright
Teacher	Servant	Cabinetmaker
Mayor	Candle maker	Cooper
Carpenter	Weaver	Barber
Gardener	Mantuamaker (dressmaker)	Printer
Cook	Musician	Bookbinder
Laundress	Jeweler	Innkeeper
Stablehand	Tailor	Minister
Baker	Pharmacist	Gaoler (jailer)
Fisherman	Doctor	Governor
Shopkeeper	Milliner (hatmaker)	Soldier
Hunter	Blacksmith	Sailor
Beekeeper	Gunsmith	

Pretend you are a young pioneer trying to decide what you want to be when you grow up. Choose four careers you might have chosen as a young pioneer. Under each occupation write a description of what you would do each day.

Write your career choice here!

_____

Write your career choice here!

_____

Write your career choice here!

_____

Write your career choice here!

_____

The Mighty Mississippi River

The Chippewa <u>Indians</u> gave the name *Messipi* to the Mississippi River which means the great river. The Mississippi is the longest river in the United States. It is 2,348 miles (6,415 km) long. Its source is a stream flowing out of Lake <u>Itaska</u> in northwestern <u>Minnesota.</u> Its beginning is so small you can easily walk across it! As it flows southward, thousands of streams and rivers join it to make it the large river it is. The Mississippi River forms all of the eastern borders for the states of Minnesota, Iowa, Missouri, Arkansas, and Louisiana and the western borders for Wisconsin, <u>Illinois,</u> Kentucky, Tennessee, and Mississippi. As the river travels, it moves faster and <u>picks up</u> and carries <u>sand</u>, mud, and <u>pebbles</u>. This is deposited as <u>silt</u> along the lower banks and in the mouth of the river. The river ends in the Gulf of Mexico.

Used the underlined words from the passage above to fill in the blanks below.

1. In what state does the Mississippi River begin?   M__ __ __ __ __ __ __ __ __
2. What is one state it borders?   I __ __ __ __ __ __ __ __
3. What is something that it carries?   S __ __ __
4. What is something it deposits?   S __ __ __
5. What is the lake's name where it begins?   I __ __ __ __ __ __
6. The river begins as a small _____?   S __ __ __ __ __ __
7. What is another word that means beginning?   S __ __ __ __ __ __
8. Who named it Messipi?   I __ __ __ __ __ __ __
9. What does it do with mud and sand?   P __ __ __ __ __ __ __ __
10. What else does it pick up?   P __ __ __ __ __ __ __
11. What is another state it borders?   I __ __ __ __

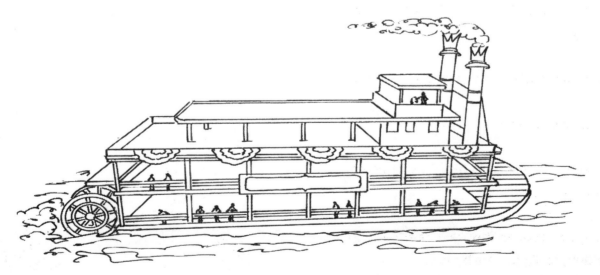

Answers: 1. Minnesota, 2. Illinois, 3. sand, 4. silt, 5. Itaska, 6. stream, 7. source, 8. Indians, 9. picks up. 10. pebbles, 11. Iowa

Wintry Weather

When Canada's cold air pushes southward and collides head-on with the warm, wet air from the Gulf of Mexico, Illinois is in for some extreme weather! The winter storm of 1837 is an example of a blizzard that caught Illinois by surprise. This weather system moved so fast that a man riding a horse was found frozen in his saddle!

Fortunately, these blizzards are rare and Illinoisans receive, on average, 38 inches (97 cm) of precipitation per year.

Pretend it is a cold, snowy January day. Help build a snowman by doing the following:

Draw a hat on the snowman and color the hat black.

Draw a red scarf around the snowman's neck.

Add two black eyes.

Add a carrot nose and color it orange.

Draw a mouth in black. Make the snowman look happy.

Put black buttons down the snowman's front.

Draw two sticks for arms.

Draw two mittens on the stick arms and color them red.

Draw a broom as though the snowman were holding it. Color the broom.

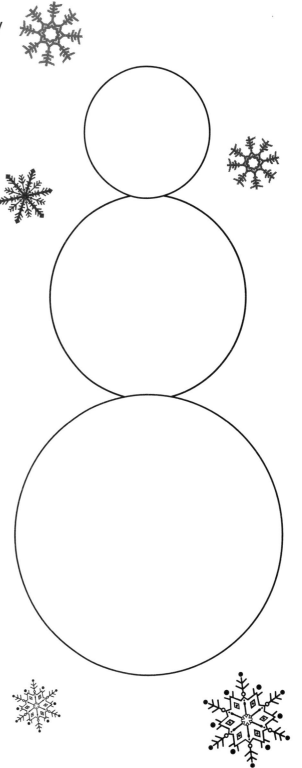

Dr. Martin Luther King, Jr.

Illinois was important in the Civil Rights movement of America. One of the leaders was a senator from Illinois named Everett Dirksen. He helped pass the Civil Rights Act of 1964 and the Voting Rights Act of 1965.

Dr. Martin Luther King, Jr. came to Chicago in 1966 to protest injustice. He wanted African-Americans to live freely anywhere in the city, not just in segregated neighborhoods. Dr. Martin Luther King, Jr. had a dream. His dream was equal rights for all Americans.

He worked very hard to make African-Americans "free at last."

Many other African-Americans made significant accomplishments for the state of Illinois, the nation, and in some cases, the world. Below are a few.

Try matching their accomplishments with their names.

_____ 1. Carol Moseley-Braun

_____ 2. John H. Johnson

_____ 3. Oprah Winfrey

_____ 4. Richard Wright

_____ 5. Mae Jemison

_____ 6. Jean Baptiste Point Du Sable

_____ 7. Harold Washington

_____ 8. Michael Jordan

_____ 9. Daniel Hale Williams

_____ 10. Andrew "Rube" Foster

A. first African-American woman elected to the U.S. Senate

B. established the first settlement in the area of Chicago

C. first African-American woman in space

D. first African-American mayor of Chicago

E. founded the most successful African-American publishing company in the world

F. Famous African-American author

G. Chicago Bulls basketball great

H. first woman, and first African-American, to own and produce her own television show

I. Chicago surgeon who improved opportunities for African-Americans in medicine

J. African-American ballplayer who organized the National Negro League

ANSWERS: 1.A, 2.E, 3.H, 4.F, 5.C, 6.B, 7.D, 8.G, 9.I, 10.J

Terrific Tracks!

Looks like the family in this snow-covered house in Illinois had some visitors during the night! See how deep the snow is? That's because there are no mountains in Illinois to block the cold winds. Because of this, the temperature can drop 20 degrees in one hour!

Can you identify the tracks below?
Draw a line from the animal to the correct set of tracks.

Black Bear   White-tailed Deer   Raccoon

Rainbow, Pretty Rainbow

Rainbows often appear over the Illinois prairie after a storm. Rainbows are formed when sunlight bends through raindrops. Big raindrops produce the brightest, most beautiful rainbows. You can see rainbows early or late on a rainy day when the sun is behind you.

Color the rainbow in the order they are listed below, starting at the top of the rainbow.

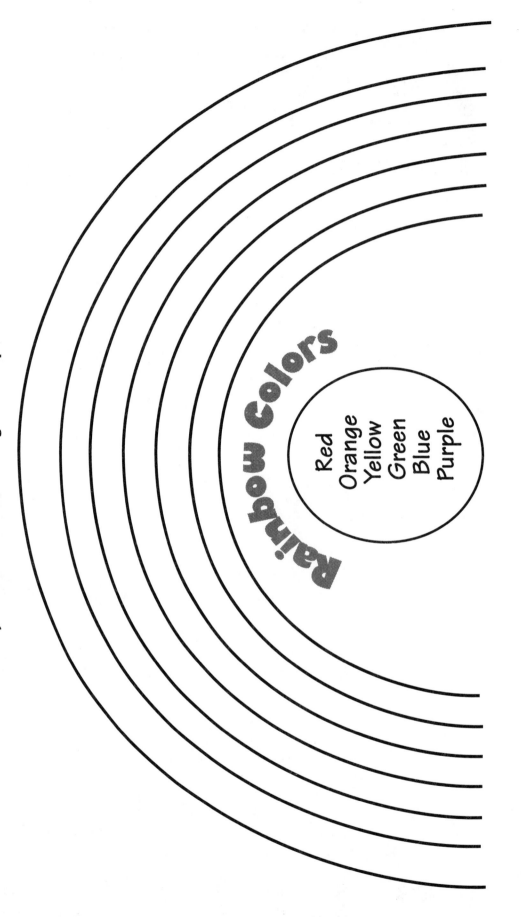

Rainbow Colors

Red
Orange
Yellow
Green
Blue
Purple

Illinois Wheel of Fortune, Indian Style!

The names of Illinois' many Native American Indian tribes contain enough consonants to play … Wheel of Fortune!

See if you can figure out the Wheel of Fortune-style puzzles below! "Vanna" has given you consonants in each word to help you out!

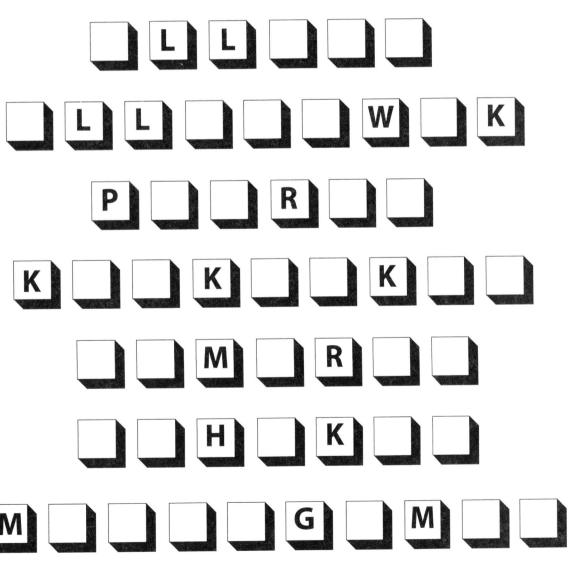

BROTHER, CAN YOU SPARE A DIME?

After the collapse of the stock market on Wall Street in 1929, the state of Illinois, along with the rest of the nation, plunged headfirst into the Great Depression. It was the worst economic crisis America had ever known. Banks closed and businesses crashed...there was financial ruin everywhere.

Our President Helps.

While the nation was in the midst of the Depression, Franklin Delano Roosevelt became president. With America on the brink of economic devastation, the federal government stepped forward and hired unemployed people to build parks, bridges and roads. With this help and other government assistance, the country began to slowly, but painfully, pull out of the Great Depression. Within his first 100 days of office, President Roosevelt enacted a number of policies to help minimize the suffering of the nation's many unemployed workers. These programs were known as the NEW DEAL. The jobs helped families support themselves and improved the country's infrastructure.

Put an X next to the jobs that were part of Roosevelt's New Deal

1. computer programmer _____

2. bridge builder _____

3. fashion model _____

4. park builder _____

5. interior designer _____

6. hospital builder _____

7. school builder _____

8. web site designer _____

9. road builder _____

Answers: 2, 4, 6, 7, 9

Illinois Writers

Fill in the missing first or last name of these famous Illinois writers.

1. First name: Ernest
   Last name: _____

2. First name: _____
   Last name: Bradbury

3. First name: Betty
   Last name: _____

4. First name: _____
   Last name: Masters

5. First name: Carl
   Last name: _____

6. First name: _____
   Last name: Brooks

7. First name: Shel
   Last name: _____ _____

To be a reader or not to be a reader -- there's only one answer!

Geographic Tools

Part 1: Beside each item, put the initials of the tool that can best help you!

(CR) Compass Rose   (LL) Longitude and Latitude
(M) Map   (G) Grid
(K) Map key/legend

1._____ I need to find the geographic location of Germany.

2._____ I need to find an airport near Springfield.

3._____ I need to find which way is north.

4._____ I need to chart a route from Illinois to California.

5._____ I need to find a small Illinois town on a map.

Part 2: Match the items on the left with the items on the right.

1. Grid system   A. Map key or legend
2. Compass rose   B. Missouri and Indiana
3. Longitude and latitude   C. A system of letters and numbers
4. Two of Illinois' borders   D. Imaginary lines around the earth
5. Symbols on a map   E. Shows N, S, E, and W

ANSWERS: 1.LL, 2.K, 3.CR, 4.M, 5.G Part 2: 1.C, 2.E, 3.D, 4.B, 5.A

Peoria Frontier Workers

Draw two pairs of shoes in the window for the shoemaker.
Draw two loaves of bread in the window of the bakery.
Draw a hammer in the blacksmith's window.
Draw a dress in the window for the dressmaker.
Draw a saddle in the saddlemaker's window.
Draw a sack of flour and a teapot in the storekeeper's window.

Blacksmith	Storekeeper	Dressmaker

Saddlemaker	Shoemaker	Bakery

Summer 1993:
Rain, Rain, Go Away!

Unscramble each word in the word bank and fill in the blanks to get all the details on this Illinois' disaster. (Some words may be used more than once.) Be sure to capitalize each word.

WORD BANK

criglrulatu
musmre
simsppsispii
ternmwiesd

rasec
gedvslaa
oparie
yemrelav
tmuaon

attse
sonlmiil
madgae
tannoi
srian

noisllii
eyra
libl tonnlic
rafrems

The mighty __ __ __ __ __ __ __ __ __ __ __ with its winding waterway has contributed to the fertile farmland of __ __ __ __ __ __ __ __. Depositing rich minerals along the banks as it travels, the __ __ __ __ __ __ __ __ __ __ __ has helped to make Illinois a major provider of __ __ __ __ __ __ __ __ __ __ __ __ products in the world. Unfortunately, though, the Mississippi has also caused devastating __ __ __ __ __ __ when its riverbanks overflow, sweeping away everything in its path. The flood of 1993 is an example of such a disaster.

During that fateful __ __ __ __ __ __ , heavy __ __ __ __ __ caused massive flooding throughout most of the __ __ __ __ __ __ __ __ __ __ United States. Large areas of Illinois were especially hard hit. Some cities, like __ __ __ __ __ __ , had more rain by the end of that July than it usually had the whole __ __ __ __ . Thousands of __ __ __ __ __ were washed away as __ __ __ __ __ __ __ watched in horror to see their livelihood destroyed before their very eyes. Small towns like __ __ __ __ __ __ __ __ had to be rebuilt after rushing walls of water swept them away. Even bridges that crossed the __ __ __ __ __ __ __ __ __ __ __ had to be closed due to the intensity and __ __ __ __ __ __ of the rainfall.

As the water finally receded, so did hopes that much could be __ __ __ __ __ __ __ __ from some of the worst flooding this __ __ __ __ __ , and region, had ever seen. Citing the __ __ __ __ __ __ __ __ of dollars estimated in property loss and devastation, President __ __ __ __ __ __ __ __ __ __ __ offered federal aid to this water-logged area of the __ __ __ __ __ __ .

ANSWERS: Mississippi, Illinois, Mississippi, agricultural, damage, summer, rains, Midwestern, Peoria, year, acres, farmers, Valmeyer, Mississippi, amount, salvaged, state, millions, Bill Clinton, nation

IT'S MONEY IN THE BANK!!

You spent the summer working at your uncle's manufacturing plant in North Chicago and you made a lot of money...$500 to be exact! Solve the problems below.

TOTAL EARNED: $500.00

I will pay back my Mom this much for money I borrowed when I first started working (Thanks Mom!): A. $20.00

subtract A ($20.00) from $500: B. _____

I will give my little brother this much money for taking my phone messages while I was at work: C. $10.00

subtract C ($10.00) from B: D. _____

I will spend this much on a special treat or reward for myself: E. $25.00

subtract E ($25.00) from D: F. _____

I will save this much for college: G. $300.00

subtract G ($300.00) from F: H. _____

I will put this much in my new savings account so I can buy school clothes: I. $100.00

subtract $100.00 from H: J. _____

TOTAL STILL AVAILABLE
(use answer J) _____

TOTAL SPENT
(add A, C, and E) _____

 # Map Symbols

Make up symbols for these names and draw them in the space provided on right.

corn	
fort	
mine	
potatoes	
pigs	
airport	
wheat	
Indian mound	

THE WHITE-TAILED DEER

Did you know that the white-tailed deer was voted the state animal by students in 1980? The deer has a gray coat in winter that turns brown in summer. The white-tailed deer was named for its bright white tail.

Unscramble these descriptive words below using the Word Bank.

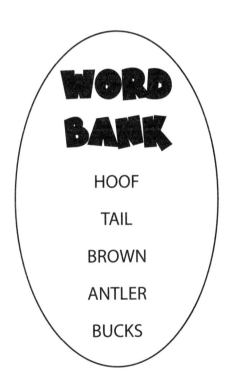

1. _ O _ L

2. _ O _ O

3. _ U _ _ O

4. _ O _ L _ _

5. _ R _ O _

Now unscramble the "bubble" letters to discover the mystery word in the sentence below:

Newborn white-tailed deer are called __ __ __ __ __

Chicago's Dino Darling

The darling of all dinosaurs is the newest mascot for the city of Chicago. Her name is Sue and she is the largest Tyrannosaurus rex (T. rex for short!) ever found. Purchased by Chicago's Field Museum at an auction in 1997, Dinosaur Sue is 41 feet long and her weight, when alive, is estimated at 7 tons. Sue's fossil skull and jaws together weigh a whopping 750 pounds! Wow, what a gal! Plans are currently underway at the museum to build a dinosaur exhibition hall, centered around Sue, scheduled to open sometime in 2003. Until then, Sue's admirers can see her at the museum's Stanley Field Hall.

Where was Sue originally found? Use this chart to "excavate" the city and state.

A	B	C	D	E	F	G	H	I	J	K	L	M	N
8	26	18	3	5	20	7	2	1	19	6	10	4	17

O	P	Q	R	S	T	U	V	W	X	Y	Z
13	22	24	9	16	11	25	15	23	12	21	14

_20_ _8_ _1_ _11_ _2_   _16_ _13_ _25_ _11_ _2_

_3_ _8_ _6_ _13_ _11_ _8_

Illinois Through the Times

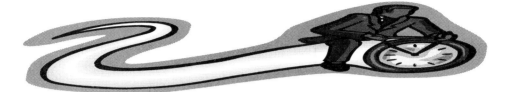

Many great things have happened in Ilinois. Chronicle the following important Illinois events by solving math problems to find out the years in which they happened.

1. Louis Jolliet and Father Jacques Marquette arrive in Illinois. 2-1=   2x3=   5+2=   9/3=

2. Illinois becomes part of the French colony of Louisiana. 6-5=   1x7=   0+1=   14/2=

3. Illinois becomes the 21st state on December 3rd. 5-4=   2x4=   9-8=   24/3=

4. The Chicago fire devastates much of the city. 7-6=   16/2=   10-3=   1x1=

5. Discontent among laborers leads to the Haymarket Square riots. 9-8=   64/8=   6+2=   2x3=

6. World's Columbian Exposition is held in Chicago. 3-2=   1x8=   3x3=   27/9=

7. Scientists at the University of Chicago control an atomic chain reaction for the first time. 8-7=   7+2=   2x2=   8/4=

8. Illinois voters approve a new constitution. 4-3=   4+5=   6+1=   5-5=

9. Jane Byrne is elected Chicago's first woman mayor. 6-5=   3+6=   21/3=   9+0=

10. Harold Washington is elected Chicago's first black mayor. 1+0=   10-1=   3+5=   9/3=

ANSWERS: 1.1673, 2.1717, 3.1818, 4.1871, 5.1886, 6.1893, 7.1942, 8.1970, 9.1979, 10.1983

People and Their Jobs!

Can you identify these people and their jobs?

Put an A by the computer technician at the Chicago Board of Trade.
Put a B by the railroad workers in Champaign-Urbana.
Put a C by the government official in Springfield.
Put a D by the coal miner in southern Illinois.
Put an E by the machinist at the John Deere Factory in Moline.
Put an F by the young farmer in Grand Detour.

Illinois State Seal

The two dates on the state seal represent the year Illinois became a state (1818) and the year the state seal was adopted (1868).

Color the state seal.

Visit the Illinois Regions

Let's visit the regions of Illinois.
Find the name of the three regions, and other unique characteristics, that make Illinois a natural beauty.

CENTRAL PLAINS

FLAT

FLOWERS

GLACIERS

GRASSES

GULF COASTAL PLAIN

HILLY

ILLINOIS RIVER

LAKE MICHIGAN

MINERALS

MISSISSIPPI

PRAIRIE

ROCK

ROCK RIVER HILLS

SHAWNEE HILLS

```
G L A C I E R S P G U L C
U S M C F L O W E R S A E
L H I K M T C R V A S K N
F A S S V F K P N S K E T
C W S X T C R R D S L M R
O N I A O T I A M E P I A
A E S R E A V I R S N C L
S E S M I N E R A L S H P
T H I N K L R I F U W I L
A I P A S P H E N S U G A
L I P E T H I L L Y V A I
P L I O L N L L T R C N N
L S V K P F L A T K C L S
A N S F T Q S V R S D B M
I L L I N O I S R I V E R
N C W O T U K M S R D W I
```

Tractors & Plows Everywhere!

Illinois is one of the nation's largest producers of farm machinery!

In 1838, John Deere, a blacksmith living in Grand Detour, Illinois, invented a new steel plow. John Deere's steel plows were a great improvement over the early iron and wood plows. They allowed farmers to clear more land much faster. Today, modern farm equipment, such as plows and tractors, has allowed Illinois farms to grow.

Color the John Deere tractor.

Also draw the background for the tractor. Illinois grows corn, soybeans, and wheat. All these can be placed in your Illinois farm picture.

Cyrus McCormick, inventor of the reaper, was honored for doing more for agriculture than any other person.

Caterpillar, the world's largest earth-moving equipment manufacturer, is also located in Illinois!

Illinois Word Wheel

Illinois WORD Wheel

Wheel labels: Chicago Fire, Peoria, Springfield, Reaper, Ohio River, Rocky Mountains, John Deere, La Salle, Ulysses S. Grant, Lincoln, Native Americans, Jefferson, Rockford, Reagan, Prairie State, Moline, Du Sable, Potawatomi, Quarter Horse, Joliet, Chicago, Illinois Ozarks, Modoc, Underground Railroad, Illinois, Black Hawk

From the Word Wheel of Illinois names and things, answer the following questions.

1. The home of the Caterpillar Tractor company is _____.

2. Home of plow-maker John Deere's largest plant is _____.

3. The Black Hawk War was the last major struggle in Illinois between _____ and the U.S. troops.

4. This French explorer traveled the length of the Mississippi River and built a fort near present-day Peoria. His name was _____.

5. The city of _____ is filled with reconstructed historic sites related to its most famous son, Abraham Lincoln.

6. A brigadier general for the Union Army, _____ was born in Galena.

7. The city that is home to the Bears, the Bulls, the Cubs, and the White Sox sports teams is _____.

8. Thieves lurked in caves along the _____.

9. The state named for the Algonquin word meaning "people" or "men" is _____.

ANSWERS: 1. Peoria, 2. Moline, 3. Native Americans, 4. La Salle, 5. Springfield, 6. Ulysses S. Grant, 7. Chicago, 8. Ohio River, 9. Illinois

Illinois Banks

Illinois banks provide essential financial services. Some of the services that banks provide include:

- They lend money to consumers to purchase goods and services such as houses, cars, and education.
- They lend money to producers who start new businesses.
- They issue credit cards.
- They provide savings accounts and pay interest to savers.
- They provide checking accounts.

Check whether you would have more, less, or the same amount of money after each event.

1. You deposit your paycheck into your checking account.   MORE   LESS   SAME

2. You put $1,000 in your savings account.   MORE   LESS   SAME

3. You use your credit card to buy new school clothes.   MORE   LESS   SAME

4. You borrow money from the bank to open a toy store.   MORE   LESS   SAME

5. You write a check at the grocery store.   MORE   LESS   SAME

6. You transfer money from checking to savings.   MORE   LESS   SAME

7. You withdraw money to buy pizza.   MORE   LESS   SAME

8. You deposit the pennies from your piggy bank.   MORE   LESS   SAME

9. You see the interest in your savings account.   MORE   LESS   SAME

10. You use the ATM machine to get money to buy a book.   MORE   LESS   SAME

Answers: 1. MORE, 2. MORE, 3. LESS, 4. LESS, 5. LESS, 6. SAME, 7. LESS, 8. MORE, 9. MORE, 10. LESS

Illinois
State Bird

Most states have a state bird. I think it reminds us that we should "fly high" to achieve our goals. The Illinois state bird is the cardinal. The cardinal is a large, red, North American songbird. Cardinals have loud cheery whistles, often heard on warm mornings. The male cardinals have bright red feathers. Female cardinals are yellowish-brown with red beaks.

Connect the dots to see a cardinal. Then color the picture.

Looking For a Home!

Match the things on the left with a home on the right!

1. antique Ferris Wheel

2. floundering fish

3. penguin

4. ship afloat

5. bald eagle

6. Mary's ghost

7. sidetracked coal car

8. soybean field

A. Lake Michigan

B. mine in southern Illinois

C. Kankakee River net

D. Resurrection Cemetery

E. John G. Shedd Aquarium

F. Upper Mississippi River National Refuge

G. Museum of Science and Industry

H. farm in Decatur

ANSWERS: 1.G, 2.C, 3.E, 4.A, 5.F, 6.D, 7.B, 8.H

A SHORT AND SWEET HISTORY OF OUR STATE

The following is a list of periods in the history of Illinois. Use an encyclopedia, almanac, or any other resource you feel is appropriate to research the periods. Write an event that occurred during each period.

Early exploration _____

Early settlement _____

American Revolution _____

Colonial era _____

Slavery era _____

Frontier era _____

Immigrants arrive _____

Great Depression _____

World War I _____

Korean War _____

World War II _____

Vietnam War _____

Civil Rights era _____

Information Age _____

Make an Illini Indian Vest!

Indians in Illinois wore clothing that was made from the skins of deer.

To make your deerskin vest, you will need a brown paper bag. Lay the bag flat, as shown in the picture. Cut out holes for your arms and neck. Make a long slit in one side of the bag.

Ideas for decorating your vest:
- glue buttons, glitter, and feathers on the vest

- use markers or crayons to draw Native American symbols on the vest

- make fringe at the bottom of the bag by snipping along the edges of the bag

- decorate your vest with beads, shells, etc.

Get together with your friends and have a great "pow-wow"!

The name, Illini, means "the people," and this is where Illinois gets its name!

Animal Scramble

Unscramble the names of these animals you might find in your Illinois backyard. Write the answers in the word wheel below the picture of each animal.

1. ***kipchnum***   Hint: She can store more than a hundred seeds in her cheeks!

2. ***ethiw dleait ered***   Hint: He raises the underside of his tail to signal danger!

3. ***nrocoac***   Hint: He has very sensitive "fingers" and uses them to find food.

4. ***ttoncoliat bitbra***   Hint: She would love to eat the cabbages in your garden!

5. ***yarg lquiersr***   Hint: He scurries around all day, burying and digging up acorns!

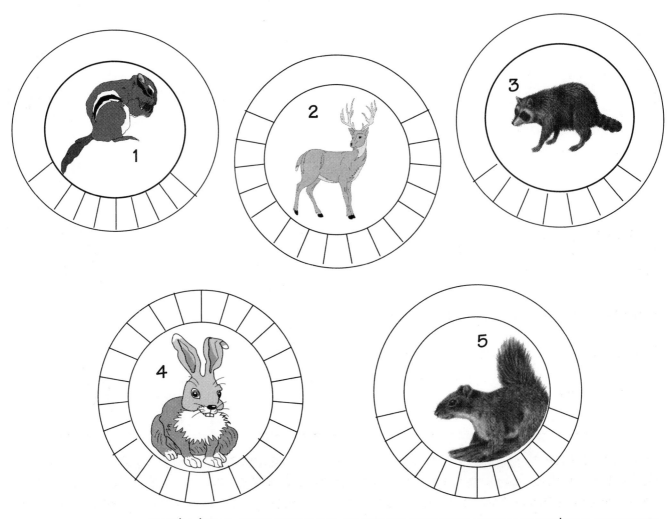

ANSWERS: 1. Chipmunk 2. White-tailed Deer 3. Raccoon 4. Cottontail Rabbit 5. Gray Squirrel

How Many People In Illinois?

STATE OF ILLINOIS

CENSUS REPORT

Every 10 years, it's time for Illinoisans to stand up and be counted. Since 1790, the United States has conducted a census, or count, of each of its citizens. Practice filling out a census form.

Name _____ Age [   ]

Place of Birth _____

Current Address _____

Does your family own or rent where you live? _____

How long have you lived in Illinois? _____

How many people are in your family? _____

How many females? [   ]   How many males? [   ]

What are their ages? _____

How many rooms are in your house? [   ]

How is your home heated? _____

How many cars does your family own? [   ]

How many telephones in your home? [   ]

Is your home a farm? _____

Sounds pretty nosy, doesn't it? But a census is very important. The information is used for all kinds of purposes, including setting budgets, zoning land, determining how many schools to build, and much more. The census helps Illinois leaders plan for the future needs of its citizens. Hey, that's you!!

Mr. Illinois, How Does Your Garden Grow?

Many Illinoisans are avid gardeners and believe gardens are important.

Can you "dig out" or "uproot" the fruits and veggies grown in Illinois?
There are 22 vegetables or fruits named here.

Can you find all of them? Write the names on the lines below.

Never disparage the asparagus! Chase the scarlet runner bean! You can't beat a beet! Do you see the broccoli? Let's lumber along the cucumber. Is that a chicken in the eggplant? Here's the beginning of the endive. I give a fig for figs! Salute the London flag leek! Toss some tennis ball lettuce in the net! Are you feeling melon, cauliflower? Oh, for some okra! Walk like an Egyptian onion! May I have some May peas, please? Bully for the bullnose pepper! Cheesecake pumpkin must make good pie! The ravishing red radish is blushing! The yellow crookneck squash has warts! The very merry strawberry is giggling. A Spanish tomato is red as a cape!

_____   _____
_____   _____
_____   _____
_____   _____
_____   _____
_____   _____
_____   _____
_____   _____
_____   _____

ANSWERS: Asparagus, Scarlet Runner Bean, Beet, Broccoli, Long Orange Carrot, Cucumber, Eggplant, Endive, Figs, London Flag Leek, Tennis Ball Lettuce, Melon, Cauliflower, Okra, Egyptian Onion, May Peas, Bullnose Pepper, Cheesecake Pumpkin, Radish, Yellow Crookneck Squash, Strawberry, Spanish Tomato

Ford-Mobile

Did you know that the Ford your family is driving today is a direct descendant of the original Model-T Ford? It's true! The Model-T was the first car to be made on the assembly line. It also was the first gasoline-powered car that sold at a price most Americans could afford! Early in his career, Henry Ford was forced into bankruptcy, but this didn't discourage him. He continued with his ideas and became a huge success. His first Model-T sold for $825! Things sure have changed! Automobiles today are still made on the assembly line… even the car you ride in. We have a lot to thank Henry Ford for… he certainly has made our lives a lot easier! Think of how much the Ford has changed from the early style of the Model-T.

Just as Ford is a direct descendant from the early automobile models, you are a direct descendant of your ancestors.

Below is a "family tree." Fill in your name as well as some of your ancestors. Ask your relatives to help you with the answers, then keep it in a safe place for future reference!

_____
Grandmother

_____
Grandfather

_____
Grandmother

_____
Grandfather

_____
Mother

_____
Father

_____
Your name here

Pioneer Corn Husk Doll

You can make a corn husk doll similar to the dolls settlers' children played with! Here's how:

You will need:
- corn husks (or strips of cloth)
- string
- scissors

1. **Select a long piece of corn husk and fold it in half. Tie a string about one inch down from the fold to make the doll's head.**

2. **Roll a husk and put it between the layers of the tied husk, next to the string. Tie another string around the longer husk, just below the rolled husk. Now your doll has arms! Tie short pieces of string at the ends of the rolled husk to make the doll's hands.**

3. **Make your doll's waist by tying another string around the longer husk.**

4. **If you want your doll to have legs, cut the longer husk up the middle. Tie the two halves at the bottom to make feet.**

5. **Add eyes and a nose to your doll with a marker. You could use corn silk for the doll's hair.**

Now you can make
a whole family
of dolls!

Please Come To Illinois

You have a friend who lives in South Carolina. She is thinking of moving to Illinois because she has heard that there is a lot of economic development in America's manufacturing belt. You want to encourage your friend to come to Illinois.

Write her a letter describing Illinois and some of the employment opportunities.

Chicago is the major financial center in the Midwest. It is home to the Chicago Board of Trade and the Chicago Mercantile Exchange. These allow people to buy and sell products and goods. Today six out of ten Illinois residents work in service industries such as medicine, finance, and education.

Lincoln's Final Journey?

After crazed actor John Wilkes Booth shot President Lincoln on April 14, 1865, the nation was stunned. When Lincoln died the next morning, plans were made to carry his body home for burial. On its mournful journey, that April of 1865, the funeral train passed through the state of New York. Since then, on days in late April, old time residents claim to see the image of this train traveling north on the tracks of the former New York Central Railroad. The ghost train has only a single flatcar with a coffin perched somberly on it. This train follows silently behind another. The front train is neatly painted and trimmed in brass. No engineers or firemen are seen on the train. A band of musicians is seen, but is not heard. Although this ghost train does not appear to match pictures of the real train, it is still recognized as a funeral train by those who see it.

To discover where the funeral train carried President Lincoln's body, circle the even number letters and list them below to complete this sentence:
President Lincoln's body was taken home

—— ————————————, —————————.

1	2	3	4	5	6	7
L	T	I	O	N	S	C
8	9	10	11	12	13	14
P	O	R	L	I	N	N
15	16	17	18	19	20	21
W	G	A	F	S	I	T
22	23	24	25	26	27	28
E	H	L	E	D	P	I
29	30	31	32	33	34	35
R	L	E	L	S	I	I
36	37	38	39	40	41	42
N	D	O	E	I	N	S

ANSWERS: TO SPRINGFIELD, ILLINOIS

Come and Get It!

Are you ready for an exciting scavenger hunt? Use your knowledge of Illinois, a friend, teacher, parent, or book to find the answers to the questions below.

On your mark, get set, get ready, GO!

1. Find the inventor of the steel plow and write his name here: ___ ___ ___ ___   ___ ___ ___ ___ ___.

2. Find where the "pirates" in Illinois hid out. ___ ___ ___ ___ - ___ ___ - ___ ___ ___ ___ ___.

3. The Illinois state bird is the ___ ___ ___ ___ ___ ___ ___ ___.

4. Which Indian tribe was forced out of Illinois by the Iroquois Indians? ___ ___ ___ ___ ___ ___ ___   ___ ___ ___ ___ ___ ___ ___.

5. Find the year that women in Illinois were allowed to vote in a presidential election: ___ ___ ___ ___.

6. A ___ ___ ___ ___ ___ ___ ___   ___ ___ ___ ___ ___ ___ ___ was hung from the door, and each young visitor was allowed to choose a Christmas treat.

7. A beautiful butterfly graces our state. Name the butterfly that is Illinois' state insect. ___ ___ ___ ___ ___ ___ ___   ___ ___ ___ ___ ___ ___ ___ ___ ___.

ANSWERS: 1. John Deere 2. Cave-in-Rock 3. Cardinal 4. Illini Indians 5. 1916 6. goodie string 7. Monarch Butterfly

Virtual Illinois!

Using your knowledge of Illinois, make a website that tells us about Illinois. You can even draw pictures of animals, places, people, etc., to make your very own website interesting. Draw your web page here.

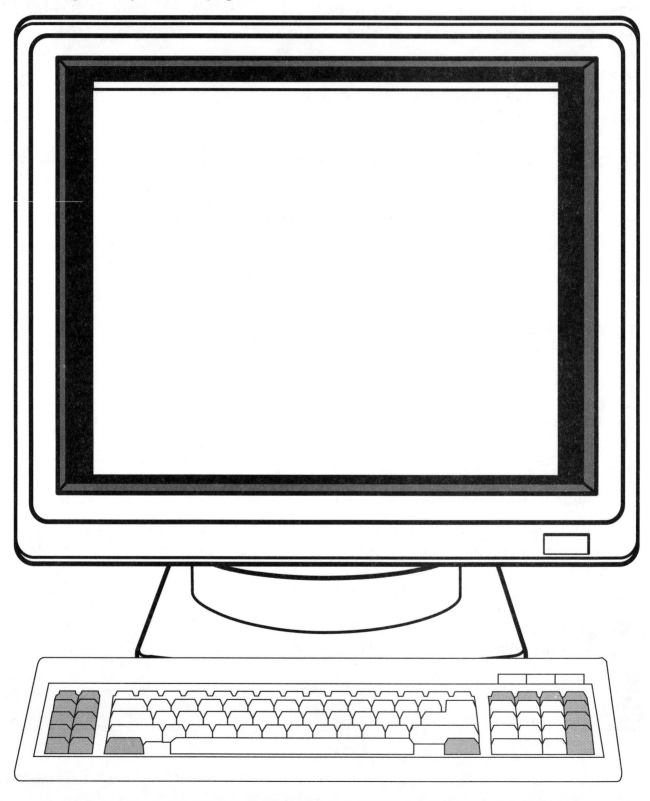

Illinois State Greats!

How many of these State Greats from the Great State of Illinois do you know?

Use an encyclopedia, almanac, or other resource to match the following facts with the State Great they describe.

Hint: there are two facts for each State Great!

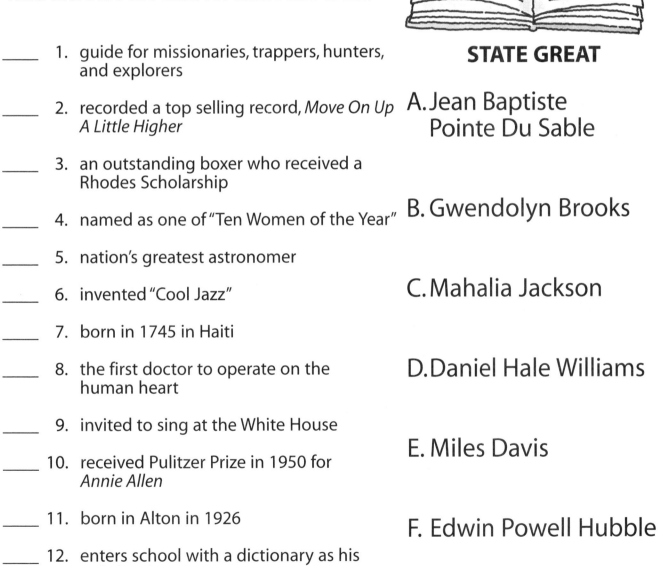

STATE GREAT

_____ 1. guide for missionaries, trappers, hunters, and explorers

_____ 2. recorded a top selling record, *Move On Up A Little Higher*

_____ 3. an outstanding boxer who received a Rhodes Scholarship

_____ 4. named as one of "Ten Women of the Year"

_____ 5. nation's greatest astronomer

_____ 6. invented "Cool Jazz"

_____ 7. born in 1745 in Haiti

_____ 8. the first doctor to operate on the human heart

_____ 9. invited to sing at the White House

_____ 10. received Pulitzer Prize in 1950 for *Annie Allen*

_____ 11. born in Alton in 1926

_____ 12. enters school with a dictionary as his only book

A. Jean Baptiste Pointe Du Sable

B. Gwendolyn Brooks

C. Mahalia Jackson

D. Daniel Hale Williams

E. Miles Davis

F. Edwin Powell Hubble

ANSWERS: 1.A, 2.C, 3.F, 4.B, 5.F, 6.E, 7.A, 8.D, 9.C, 10.B, 11.E, 12.D

The Scenic Route

Imagine that you are leading a tour to famous Illinois' cities and landmarks. Circle the following places on the map below, then number them in the order which you would visit them, north to south.

Little America _____

East St. Louis _____

Charles Mound _____

Abraham Lincoln's home _____

Chicago _____

Shawnee National Forest _____

Honest Abe Lincoln

Most historians consider Abraham Lincoln to be America's greatest president. His speeches made him a national political figure. Lincoln's "House Divided" speech, as well as his "Gettysburg Address," are among his best remembered and people quote them to this day. He is a perfect example of how much the "self-educated" man can achieve. He was a pioneer in civil rights with his Emancipation Proclamation, and he took the first step toward ending the injustice of slavery. Even today, Lincoln is still revered as an honest and ethical man and a true American hero!

Cross out every other letter below beginning with the second one. The letters that remain will answer the questions.

HHOLUBSTEM DEITVMITDREBDL

In a famous speech Lincoln said a "_ _ _ _ _ _ _ _ _ _ _ _ _ _ against itself cannot stand."

TRWMOP MLIGNFURTZETSA

Even though Lincoln's speeches have endured, they did not necessarily last a long time. His Gettysburg Address lasted _ _ _ _ _ _ _ _ _ _ _ _.

ECTBHRITCLSM HMOTNREZSXTBYB

Lincoln is remembered for his _ _ _ _ _ _ and _ _ _ _ _ _ _ _.

GLERTATXYCSTBGUBRCG AGDBDARBERSMST

Lincoln's _____ _____ outlined the importance of the Civil War.

SAECLBFX ELDGURCDABTMEODQ

Instead of going to school, Lincoln was _____ _____.

ANSWERS: HOUSE DIVIDED, TWO MINUTES, ETHICS, HONESTY, GETTYSBURG ADDRESS, SELF EDUCATED

What's In The Bag?

Find something at home that is symbolic of the great state of Illinois! Place it in a bag (to keep it a secret). Write some clues about your item on this sheet. Read them to a friend to see if they can guess "what's in the bag"!

CLUES:

_____

_____

_____

_____

_____

_____

_____

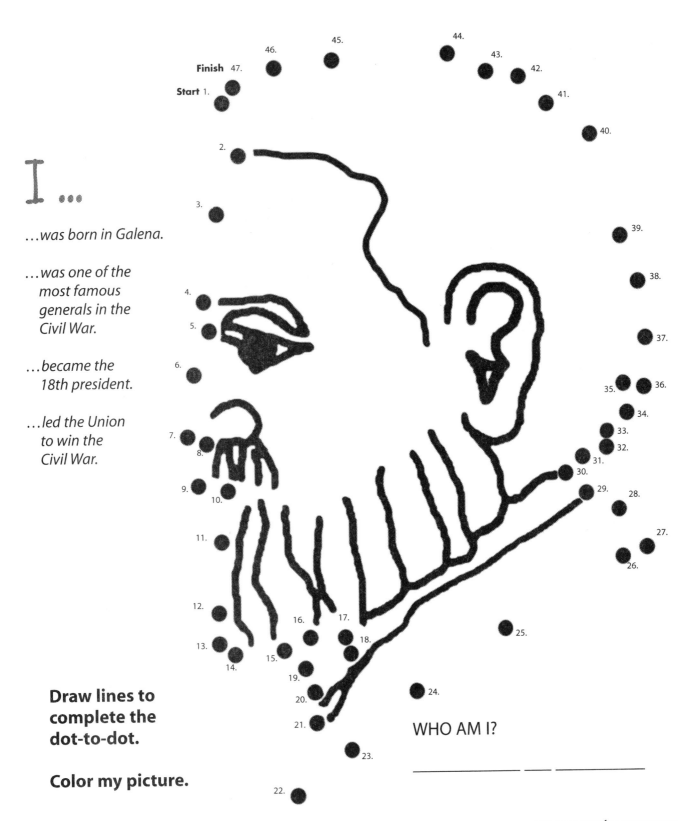

I ...

...*was born in Galena.*

...*was one of the most famous generals in the Civil War.*

...*became the 18th president.*

...*led the Union to win the Civil War.*

Draw lines to complete the dot-to-dot.

Color my picture.

WHO AM I?

_____ ___ _____

ANSWER: Ulysses S. Grant

Would You Know Woodhenge?

While exploring the Cahokia Mounds in Illinois, archaeologists found a circle of holes in the ground. These curious holes apparently once held wooden posts. What would they have been used for by the native peoples who lived there around 900 AD (CE)?

The mysterious ring of posts may have been the site of sacred ceremonies. It also might have served as an astronomical calendar. This strange place reminds archaeologists of Stonehenge, an ancient site in England that has a ring of enormous stones. Because Stonehenge continues to baffle scientists, it was decided to name this interesting Illinois site "Woodhenge."

Draw your version of Woodhenge below as it might have appeared in the past. Is a sacred ceremony in progress? Or is the ring of wooden posts an astronomical calendar? Something else? You decide!

Let's Have Words!

Make as many words as you can from the letters in the words

Land of Lincoln

_____   _____   _____

_____   _____   _____

_____   _____   _____

_____   _____   _____

_____   _____   _____

_____   _____   _____

_____   _____   _____

_____   _____   _____

_____   _____   _____

_____   _____   _____

_____   _____   _____

_____   _____   _____

Grandma Minnie's Quilting Bee

Once upon a time, Grandma Minnie lived in a tiny house near Chicago. "This is where our history began," she would always say, "and we must preserve it." Grandma Minnie loved to quilt and made beautiful patchwork quilts. Sometimes she would quilt at home in her sewing room and sometimes with her friends at quilting bees.

Match the items from Grandma Minnie's sewing room and quilting bee.

thimble

thread

pins

scissors

needle

cat

rocking chair

trunk

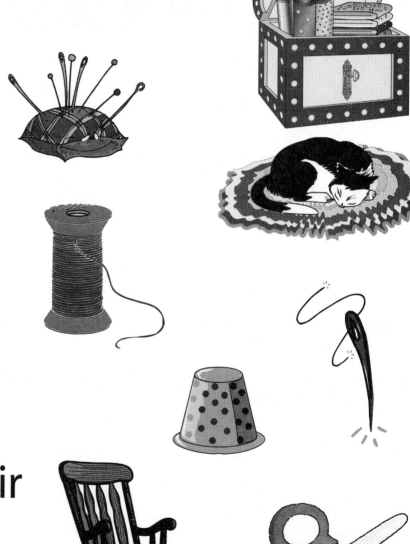

Mrs. O'Leary's Cow

Chicago was a growing city when it was almost completely devastated by a fire on October 8, 1871! According to legend, the fire was started when Mrs. O'Leary's cow kicked over a lantern. The story is most likely not true. Whatever happened, the fire destroyed much of the central city, took 300 lives, and left 100,000 people homeless. After a new beginning, the city was inspired to even greater achievements.

There are many myths and legends throughout history. A *myth* is a story that involves gods and heroes and explains something a culture practices. It can also be about an event, such as the cow who kicked over a lantern. This is a tough question so think hard …

Can you create a myth in three lines? You can make one up based on current events.

_____

_____

_____

A *legend* is a story that cannot be proven to be based on history or the truth. It is handed down through tradition.

Write two or more lines that read like a legend. Again, you can make this up using your imagination.

_____

_____

_____

_____

Mmmm?!
Fact or Fiction?

Famous Illinois People Scavenger Hunt

Here is a list of just some of the famous people from our state. Go on a scavenger hunt to see if you can "capture" a fact about each one. Use an encyclopedia, almanac, or other resource you might need. Happy hunting!

FAMOUS PERSON   **FAMOUS FACT**

Franklin Pierce Adams   _____
Jane Addams   _____
Mary Astor   _____
Jack Benny   _____
Black Hawk   _____
Harry Blackmun   _____
Ray Bradbury   _____
William Jennings Bryan   _____
Edgar Rice Burroughs   _____
Gower Champion   _____
John Chancellor   _____
Raymond Chandler   _____
Jimmy Connors   _____
James Gould Cozzens   _____
Richard J. Daley   _____
Miles Davis   _____
Betty Friedan   _____
Benny Goodman   _____
Wild Bill Hickok   _____
Keokuk   _____
Archibald MacLeish   _____
William S. Paley   _____
Ronald Reagan   _____
Carl Sandburg   _____
Irving Wallace   _____
Florenz Ziegfield   _____

Illinois
People

A state is not just towns and mountains and rivers. A state is its people! But the really important people in a state are not famous. You may know them—they may be your mom, your dad, or your teacher. The average, everyday person is the one who makes the state a good state. How? By working hard, by paying taxes, by voting, and by helping Illinois' children grow up to be good state citizens!

Match each Illinois person with their accomplishment.

1. Olof Krans
2. George Rogers Clark
3. Gwendolyn Brooks
4. Richard J. Daley
5. Jane Byrne
6. Carl Sandburg
7. William Wrigley, Jr.
8. Stephen A. Douglas
9. Harold Washington
10. Edgar Lee Masters
11. Clarence Darrow
12. Betty Friedan

A. wrote *The Spoon River Anthology*

B. first elected woman mayor (1979)

C. Bishop Hill's famous folk artist

D. political opponent of Lincoln

E. author and feminist

F. longest time served as mayor of Chicago

G. led battles in Kaskaskia and Cahokia

H. famous poet - wrote about Chicago

I. one of the state's finest poets

J. manufacturer of chewing gum

K. first African-American mayor (1983)

L. famous lawyer

I wrote a poem!

ANSWERS: 1.C 2.G 3.I 4.F 5.B 6.H 7.J 8.D 9.K 10.A 11.L 12.E

Illinois Gazetteer

A gazetteer is a list of places. Use the word bank to complete the names of some of these famous places in our state:

1. Cahokia __ __ __ __ __ __

2. __ __ __ __ __ __ River

3. Mississippi __ __ __ __ __

4. St. Lawrence __ __ __ __ __ __

5. Quad __ __ __ __ __ __

6. __ __ __ __ __ __ International Airport

7. State __ __ __ __ __ __

8. Illinois __ __ __ __ __ __ __ Railroad

9. Cave-in- __ __ __ __

10. __ __ __ __ __ __ __ __ State Fair

Word Bank

Cities
Central
Rock
Mounds
DuQuoin
Seaway
O'Hare
Wabash
River
Street

Answers: 1. Mounds, 2. Wabash, 3. River, 4. Seaway, 5. Cities, 6. O'Hare, 7. Street, 8. Central, 9. Rock, 10. DuQuoin

Illinois
Trivia

Did you know that the typical Illinois farm has 370 acres (148 hectares)? That's a lot of land!

Walt Disney, the master cartoonist, was born in Illinois. Have you ever visited Disney World or Disneyland?

A department store that you find at many malls, Sears, Roebuck and Company, started in Chicago as a mail-order business.

Many of the foods you eat and use every day are packaged in Illinois. Some examples are breakfast cereal, candy, cakes, butter, cheese, flour, corn syrup, and even the pet food your cat or dog eats!

If you took all the ears of corn that are grown in Illinois every year and placed them end to end, they would stretch from Earth to the planet Venus!

The southern third of Illinois was nicknamed Egypt by the pioneers because they thought it looked like the African country of Egypt.

Prehistoric Indians in Illinois hunted mastodons for dinner!

The Temple Mound builders, a once flourishing Indian culture between A.D. (CE) 900 and 1300, built Monk's Mound which covered close to 17 acres (6.8 hectares).

The town of Kaskaskia was washed away by Mississippi River floods, not once but twice. The first time was in 1844 then again in 1881. Both times the town had to be rebuilt.

A fact I know: _____

_____

Illuminating Illinois!

All of the following were invented in Illinois for life "on the lighter side."

Complete the rhymes and riddles.

1. Today they're "in-line," smooth-rolling, and have brakes
   Before them came the ball-bearing roller _ _ _ _ _ _.

2. You buy a ticket, stand in line, what a deal!
   To ride high in the sky on a _ _ _ _ _ _ _ _ _ _ _ _ _.

3. It lights up, has bumpers, bells, and sound
   And stands on tall legs up off the ground.
   What is it? _ _ _ _ _ _ _ _ _ _ _ _ _ _ _ _ _.

4. This one is work and I know it sounds mean,
   It works by suction and helps you clean.
   What is it? _ _ _ _ _ _ _ _ _ _ _ _ _ _ _ _ _.

5. Long ago they closed things with a hook and eye
   Now they use a _ _ _ _ _ _ _ to make clothes comply!

6. The bicycle from Freeport can be taken from the rack
   And stopped quickly by merely pedaling _ _ _ _ _.

7. Put in money, step up to see what you weigh,
   Then return to the machine the very next day.
   Step up again, but don't turn pale,
   When you hear your weight
   from a _ _ _ _ _ _ _ _ _ _ _ _ _ _ _ _!

> **DID YOU KNOW?**
> Crackerjack popcorn was invented in the mid-1890s in Chicago!

ANSWERS: 1. skates, 2. ferris wheel, 3. pinball machine, 4. vacuum cleaner, 5. zipper, 6. back, 7. talking scale

Cows on Parade

Are you a lover of cows? Do you like to paint and decorate? In 1999, there was an exhibition called Cows on Parade in downtown Chicago where unpainted cows were put on display. Visitors could purchase an unpainted cow and submit a design for their new "pet." They then painted and decorated the cow. The final "dressed up" herd remained on display and later went on "tour" around the nation. At the end of the exhibition, selected cows were sold at auction, and the proceeds went to a charity picked by the cow's owner! Isn't that a unique and fun fund-raising idea?

Below is your cow for the parade. Color, paint, or decorate her for the auction. Remember, the most unusual ones bring the most money!

Illinois
Annual Events

You can visit a festival every month of the year in Illinois! Even the winter months have the Winter Carnival in Galena, the Lake Shelbyville Festival of Lights, and a Christmas Around the World Display at the Museum of Science and Industry in Chicago. Summer festivals include the Grape Festival in Nauvoo, the Apple Festival in Long Grove, Steamboat Days in Peoria, A Taste of Chicago, plus many others.

Circle the items you might find at a festival or event in Illinois.

Zoo Run!

Slip on your sneakers and let's go. We're taking a 2K run through the Brookfield Zoo today! Let's go see the new arrivals: a polar bear, llama, cow, spider monkeys, and pygmy goats! The zoo is proud of its work on behalf of the animals here. The zoo can also help us learn about animals, conservation, the natural world, and what we can do to make a difference.

Name these animals you might find at the Zoo.

_____

_____

_____

ANSWERS: lion, monkey, parrot, elephant, bear, giraffe, penguin, alligator, flamingo

You've Got Mail!

Send an e-mail to the past. E-mail a boy or girl from early Illinois and tell them what they are missing in today's world.

WRITE   SAVE   SEND   DELETE   INTERNET
NEWS AND NOTES

And, who knows? You may even get a message in return... a message written on parchment with a quill pen telling you what you are missing from a simpler time!

Bio Bottles

Biography bottles are 2 or 3 liter bottles, emptied and cleaned. They are then decorated like your favorite Illinois character. They can be someone from the past or the present such as Black Hawk, Ernest Hemingway, or Jackie Joyner-Kersee. Use your imagination!

Here are some items you may want to help you:

2 or 3 liter bottles

scissors

glue

felt

balloon or styrofoam ball for head

paint

yarn for hair

What Did We Do Before Money?

In very early America, there were no banks. However, people still wanted to barter, trade, or otherwise "purchase" goods from each other.

Wampum, made of shells, bone, or stones, was often swapped for goods. Native Americans, especially, used wampum for "money."

The barter system was when people swapped goods or services. "I'll give you a chicken if you bake me some bread."

Later, banks came into existence, and people began to use money to buy goods. However, they still bartered when they had no money to spend.

Look at the pictures below. Number them in order from 1 to 3, to tell which method was used by early Americans to purchase goods and services.

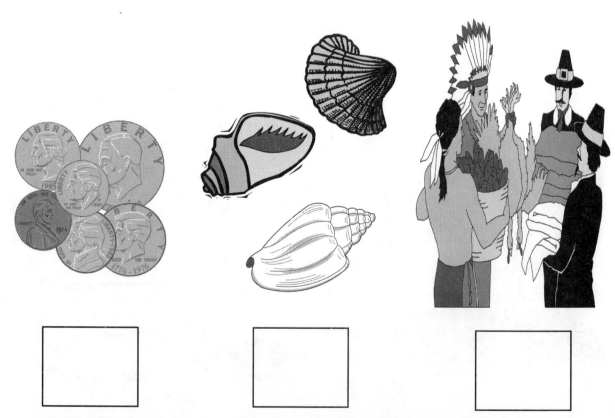

Illinois,
A Quilt of Many Counties

Illinois has 95 counties. To make a "quilt" of your state, use different colored markers or crayons to shade in the counties. Write in the name of your county, town, and your state's capital.

WOW!
What a colorful quilt!

Unique Illinois Place Names

Can you match the double-word names of these Illinois cities and towns?

1. Starved Rock
2. Buffalo Rock
3. Cahokia Mounds
4. Cave-in-Rock
5. Fort Defiance
6. Rock Island
7. New Salem
8. Shawnee Hills

A. The largest remaining prehistoric earthwork in North America
B. One of the four quad cities
C. Abraham Lincoln lived here; after he left, it became a ghost town
D. Area in the southern tip of Illinois
E. Site of an Indian tragedy; a 130 foot rock above the Illinois River
F. A restored coal mine that is now a state park
G. Hideout for river pirates
H. Center of Union Army activity during the Civil War

The Name Game!!

ANSWERS: 1.E, 2.F, 3.A, 4.G, 5.H, 6.B, 7.C, 8.D

U.S. Time Zones

Would you believe that the continental United States is divided into four time zones? It is! Because of the rotation of the earth, the sun travels from east to west. Whenever the sun is directly overhead a city, we call that time noon. But, when it is noon in Peoria, the sun has a long way to go before it is directly over, say, Sacramento, California. In other words, it can't be noon in every place at the same time! This explains the reason the continental United States has four time zones. For example, when it is 12:00 pm (noon) in Miami, it is 11:00 am in Chicago, Illinois. Did you notice there is a one-hour time difference between each zone?

Look at the time zones on the map below, then answer the following questions:

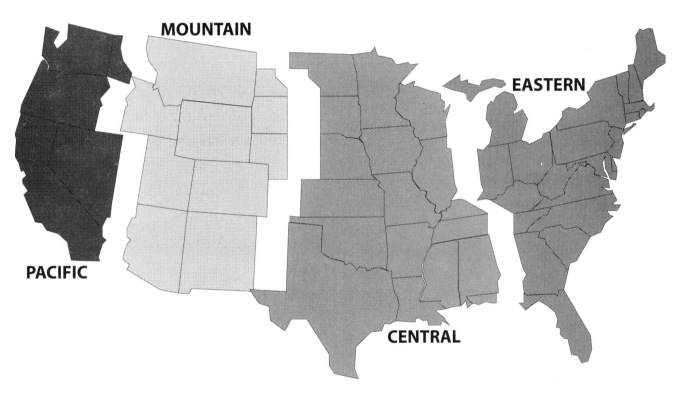

1. When it is 10:00 am in Springfield, Illinois what time is it in Georgia? _____ am

2. When it is 3:30 pm in Peoria, Illinois what time is it in Kansas? _____ pm

3. What time zone is Illinois located in? _____

4. What time zone is California in? _____

5. If it is 10:00 pm in Aurora, Illinois, what time is it in California? _____ pm

Answers: 1. 10:00 am, 2. 3:30 pm, 3. Central, 4. Pacific, 5. 8:00 pm

Illinois State Song

The beautiful lyrics of "Illinois" are rich with meaning.

See if you can match the underlined lyrics with something from the match-up list.
Write your choice on the line next to its lyric. Don't forget to check your answers!

"Illinois"
Words by C.H. Chamberlain,
Music by Archibald Johnston

From a wilderness of prairies,
Straight thy way and never varies,
_____ Till upon the <u>inland sea,</u>
_____ Stands thy <u>great commercial tree,</u>
    turning all the world to thee.

(Refrain)
By thy river gently flowing, Illinois, Illinois
O'er thy prairies verdant growing, Illinois, Illinois,
Comes and echo on the breeze,
Rustling through the leafy trees, and its mellow
    tones are these, Illinois, Illinois
And its mellow tones are these, Illinois

_____ <u>When you heard your country calling,</u>
_____ <u>Where the shot and shell were falling,</u>
_____ When the <u>southern host withdrew,</u>
_____ <u>Pitting Gray against the Blue,</u>
_____ There were none more brave than <u>you.</u> (Refrain)

Not without thy wondrous story,
Can be writ the nation's glory,
On the record of thy years,
_____ <u>Abraham Lincoln's</u> name appears,
_____ Grant and <u>Logan,</u> and our tears. (Refrain)

MATCH-UP LIST

A. people of Illinois

B. Confederate against Union

C. 16th President

D. battlefields

E. Illinois governor

F. Mississippi River

G. White oak

H. joining Civil War

I. Confederate army pulls back

Illinois Timeline: A Short & Sweet History Of Our State

The varied time periods of Illinois' timeline have added to the richness of its history.

Look at the mixed-up timeline below and put the time periods in their correct chronological order. Number them from 1 to 10 with 1 being the first time period occurring in Illinois history. The first two have been done for you.

_____ mid 1800s famous Lincoln and Douglas debate

___1___ late 1600s Jolliet and Marquette arrive in Illinois

_____ early 1870s the Chicago Fire destroys much of the city

___2___ early 1800s Illinois becomes the 21st state

_____ early 1970s the people of Illinois get new Constitution

_____ mid 1880s Haymarket Riots in Chicago

_____ late 1980s Governor James R. Thompson elected to a record fourth term

_____ early 1900s the Chicago River is made to flow backwards by the completion of Chicago Sanitary and Ship Canal

_____ early 1890s the World's Columbian Exposition held in Chicago

_____ early 1940s University of Chicago scientists control atomic chain reaction

You can do it – First to last, end with present – start with past!

ANSWERS: 3, 1, 4, 2, 9, 5, 10, 7, 6, 8

Save the Birds!

Illinois lies in the Mississippi Flyway, a route followed by millions of birds during spring and fall migrations. Species of waterfowl commonly seen in the state during the migrations include the Canada goose, common merganser, pintail, lesser scaup, shoveler, blue-wing teal, green-wing teal, ruddy duck, and mallard. Some migrant waterfowl, such as the mallard, breed and nest in Illinois if conditions permit. Upland game birds include the ring-necked pheasant, woodcock, northern bobwhite, and wild turkey. Among other birds found in the state are the meadowlark, robin, flicker, herring gull, American crow, blue jay, white-breasted nuthatch, starling, ruby-throated hummingbird, and cardinal (the state bird).

Begin by making a bird feeder, then sit back and enjoy the beauty of birds as they fly in for a snack.

Materials:

1 empty, clean 1/2 gallon orange juice carton
1 pair of pointed, sharp scissors
1 wooden stick or tree limb, 10 to 12 inches long
1 large paper clip
1 bag of birdseed
1 six inch piece of yarn or string

Instructions:

1. With sharp scissors, cut doors in the center of carton, leaving 1/2" to 1" border.
2. Cut a small 1/2" hole underneath both door frames, then slide stick through the holes to create a perch.
3. Open paper clip to make hook, then make a small hole at the top of carton and push hook through opening.
4. Add birdseed to feeder.
5. String yarn through top of hook and tie feeder to tree branch making sure it is safe from predators.